GET
Indie Artists
SIGNED
IN SYNC

MW01230568

John Clinebell & Sonnet Simmons
Foreword by Josh Young

TABLE OF CONTENTS

STORIES

FOREWORD

By Josh Young

Founder and CEO of Atrium Music

I have always had a love for music, and one of my favorite things to do is to share my passion with others at songwriting conferences. I had been to this particular one many times. It was up in beautiful Northern California. It was a Saturday morning, and I had a couple of panels and a few song screenings. At one screening, I saw a name on the list; I recognized it immediately. It was a name I hadn't seen since high school. When it was her turn, she brought up her CD to the front of the room where I was sitting, along with a note that read, "Please don't make me cry." I didn't know what to think, I worried, "Oh no, how bad is this song going to be? Is she worried that I will judge her because I knew her all those years ago? Or does she expect me to go easy on her?"

So I put in the CD, turned it on and waited... The song started playing and I started to smile. It turns out it was terrific. And that note that Sonnet Simmons had given me along with the CD wasn't a note at all, it was the name of the song.

Looking back twenty-five years ago, who would imagine a songwriters conference would reintroduce two old high school friends? How crazy to think we both would be working in the same world of sync.

I met John Clinebell more traditionally—by 'way of fellow musicians.' He had been a co-writer with one of our artists. Since then he has written dozens of tracks for us, many of which we've placed on popular shows.

In the music industry, which I saw firsthand growing up, it has always been, and still is today, a cutthroat culture. No surprise there. Musicians have never wanted to share much about what they were learning, job opportunities, or anything. Many times the excuse for screwing someone over is because it's the "music business." This has never sat well with me. I think people should come first and have been lucky enough to have met so many successful individuals who think the same way. Yes, it is a business, but building relationships and more importantly building individuals up, is instrumental. Specifically, in the sync world I have been so lucky to have met many who actually love what they do, are grateful for the career paths they have been on, and want to share everything with everyone.

When Atrium was started, we wanted to build a business that was open and transparent to the artists so they could feel comfortable in this business which was new, big, and scary. We decided we would set out to share and teach everything we knew to anyone willing to listen. We wanted to let artists be artists and give them as much knowledge as possible.

In the last 5 years, there have been more resources available than ever before. Sonnet and John's music business coaching company, 2Indie, has stood out among them all. The information, of course, is vital, but the community and positive support that John and Sonnet have created is just awesome. I think it is important to build people up in as many ways as possible in life. I will tell you I have not seen that more than with John and Sonnet. Every event they have, every education session, and the community that they have built are so kind and supportive of artists and composers at every level. I have been asked many times to speak on and run panels for 2Indie, and I always walk away feeling inspired to do more. Yes, the music in their community is quite good, the talent is growing and the teaching is strong, but the people are great.

This book is another example of the generosity of knowledge that Sonnet and John are sharing with artists who are looking to jump into the world of sync. They have laid it out incredibly well and simply. For a business that is so complicated, this book is easy to understand.

I think anyone who is getting started in the world of sync, or even if you have been making a living at it for a while, this book will help guide you. It is packed with so much vital information.

This is the kind of book you keep on your desk and look at every time you are signing with a new publisher or sync agent, are sitting down to write a new song with some fellow songwriters, or are just getting ready to hand your CD to some guy at a songwriting conference to get their feedback in hopes to get your song placed.

INTRO

In recent years, many indie artists all around the world have thought to themselves: "I make music. How do I get it used on TV and get paid for that? Who are the best people to help me?" This book's primary aim is to answer this question and help set you on a fast track to getting your music repped for licensing opportunities in media.

We want to preface the entire book by stating that the media industry is *always* changing. While the concepts and information contained in this book should remain accurate for the foreseeable future, it's entirely possible that new technologies, trends, or laws could flip portions of the industry on its head. Being connected to the larger sync community is the best insurance against this. We recommend staying tuned to the Music Licensing Podcast (MusicLicensingPodcast.com) for weekly conversations involving the latest sync industry news. And yes, we host it!

We've been helping indie artists learn how to license their music since 2016, when Sonnet started with Catch The Moon Music (CTM), running the licensing agency and teaching for Cathy Heller. In 2018, John hopped on CTM's coaching staff. By late 2019, we were both teaching full-time and running CTM's licensing agency, which gave us the chance to pitch the music of our students, as well as other established artists on the roster like The Highfields, Locksley, and Kyler England.

While running Catch the Moon Music's boutique music licensing agency, we landed high-profile placements with brands like McDonald's, Miller Lite, American Eagle, Tommy Hilfiger, Chico's, MaxMara, Signet Jewelers, Nordstroms, and networks like ABC, E!, MTV, Paramount+, Hulu, Prime, & The CW. At the same time, we created personal relationships with music supervisors and advertising agencies around the world.

The purpose of this book is to share the insights we've gleaned from years of running a sync agency, landing hundreds of media placements of our music, and teaching tens of thousands of indie artists how to license theirs. We share our experience in licensing and what we've learned from years of meetings and interviews with top music supervisors, sync agency reps, ad agency creatives, and major studio execs.

Though you'll find lots of legal pointers in this book, we are not entertainment lawyers in any way. You'll *always* want to refer to an actual attorney when it comes time for you to make important decisions like signing a split sheet, rep deal, or a license agreement.

The main points we aim to get across in the book are reinforced throughout by quotes from sync agency reps we have built relationships with. We also incorporate our own stories as independent music makers in sync throughout the book.

Ultimately, we hope that this book invigorates you with the possibility of what you can achieve with your music, reminds you that your music matters, and that you are not alone on this journey. We hope it helps you feel supported and guided in your music career as we pull back the curtain on the "mysterious" world of sync and give you actionable steps that you can take to get your songs repped by sync agencies.

This book is our letter of appreciation to all the indie artists, songwriters, and producers out there trying to make a difference in the world with their art. Your music adds to the vibrant fabric of today's industry landscape. In a hyper-competitive market like ours, it's important to find creative avenues through which your songs can be heard and appreciated by the masses. Music licensing offers you a wide variety of opportunities to reach a bigger audience and actually be paid for it. While the business of sync can be challenging to grasp, it remains one of the most worthwhile avenues for music makers to invest their time and energy into. Okay, let's dig in, friends!

John & Sonnet

THE OPPORTUNITY OF SYNC

There are more forms of media today than ever before. Most of it strategically incorporates music to enhance the message being delivered on screen. Licensing your music to media projects like commercials, shows, and films presents you with the opportunity to gain a larger audience while also getting paid to do it.

"For some indie artists, sync is a more flexible alternative to gigging and touring, with the ability to work from anywhere and create one's schedule. For others, it's a more appealing prospect than navigating the world of Spotify algorithms and social media followers. Some artists are doing all of the above, while also exploring sync as an additional revenue stream. When an artist's priorities and strengths align with the business of sync, it can be a practical way to find success in the music industry."

Brad Cryan, Production Manager
411 Music Group

When you license your songs, the production company or ad agency that syncs your music doesn't permanently own your music. Much like having a driver's license allows you to legally take a car out onto the roads, music licenses grant companies legal permission to use your songs for a specific purpose and period.

After a company has received permission to use your music in their media project, they will use your music according to the agreed-upon terms in the licensing agreement. Once the finished product is publicly released, the potential is there for millions of people to hear your music. Some will seek you out and become fans. And remember, because you didn't sell the song outright, you can have that same song licensed over and over again. Getting paid each time it lands another sync.

"Besides obviously being a way to make money as an indie artist - sync can also really help build a fanbase. Sync can act as a great aggregator of music - it's a great discovery tool for people. I recently landed a song in a big, buzzy Netflix show for one of our bands. They were SO excited! Invited all their friends and family over to have a premiere of the episode only to realize as they watched it that it was a deep background use. When they wrote to me later, they were still excited (and thrilled with the money) but I could tell they were a little disappointed that the use wasn't more featured on the show. However - that slight disappointment quickly turned to elation as they were included on the show's official Spotify playlist. The song went from around 1000 plays to over 600,000 plays in a few months. They've garnered fans for life - who will now check out every new release they ever put into the world because of that."

John Newcomer,
Creative Sync / Digital Content Manager
Bank Robber Music

When indie artists find consistent success in sync, it's because they understand how music gets placed, know how to pitch their music effectively and have a highly desirable sound that brands and networks want to exchange their clout and money for.

A Happy Feeling

It was a scorching day in early May near the Mojave Desert in 2017. Nothing but sun, blue skies, and miles of open terrain lay ahead of me as I was driving from Los Angeles to Phoenix on the I-10 Highway. Right before the California/Arizona border, I decided to pull into a truck stop. You know, the ones that have showers, video game arcades, and a whole aisle devoted to beef jerky. I walked in and started grabbing a drink. I was filling up a cup at the soda dispenser when I heard my voice from across the room. I look above the dollar-eating claw game machine to a TV that's mounted to the ceiling. I was amazed to realize that a Starbucks commercial was playing on the screen, and I could hear my voice singing the cheery lines of a song of mine titled "Happy Feeling": "Hey ho / wanna wonder why / something really got me feelin' fine / okay, all I gotta say / happy is a honey sunny place."

At that moment, it hit home that what I had been working hard for over a year to achieve had actually happened. Sure, I had previously gotten a call from Music Alternatives telling me that the deal went through. The jump up and down excitement, the calling all my friends and family, the high fives with my collaborators. But this was my "hearing yourself on the radio for the first time" kind of moment. I knew right then that my voice was being heard by millions of people. It made me so happy to know that the authentically positive song I had helped write was helping to make people's day. I was now a sonic contributor to the fabric of daily life for people. And getting paid so well for it! I'll never forget the check that I got in the mail. It was the most money I'd ever made doing anything in my life.

Sync has the power to greatly impact people's lives. It can quickly check off bucket list items for indie artists.

Change someone's music career overnight. Or act in more subtle ways as a real long-term earning stream for music makers around the world. You can find a home in sync, create lifelong friendships, and find the true creative voice you've been looking for your whole life. All in the noble pursuit of making shows, movies, games and so many other types of media their most powerful. What a rewarding journey it can be. I'm so glad I jumped into some music licensing workshops and took what I learned to heart. That's my advice to anyone who's starting in sync!

One Little Lyric Edit Can Change Everything

I landed my first sync fortuitously in 2008 for an amusement park and Coca-Cola commercial. The agency producing the commercial was looking on YouTube for covers of the song "Summertime" and found a version with me singing it. They reached out to see if I would record it for the commercial. However, they came to find that the clearance for "Summertime" was out of their budget. Lucky for me, they came back to me and asked what other songs I might have that they could listen to, that might work for the commercial.

It was early in my songwriting days. I wrote mostly songs about heartbreaks, and I had just written a song called "You're No Good For Me." That was one of the only finished songs I had to send them. I got out my keyboard and voice recorder on my phone to send them a demo. As I was about to record, I had this little thought, "Would the lyrics NO GOOD FOR ME, work for a commercial? Maybe I should change that?" And so I did. I changed it to "You're SO good for me." I didn't change any other lyrics in the song but that one word and sent it over. The demo included my dog Sasha and her collar jingling in the background, the new lyric, and me just singing into my phone voice recorder.

The producer of the commercial loved the song, the brands loved the song, and it was picked for the commercial spots. A little miracle indeed.

I had no idea what a stir the song would cause. One of the local news stations in Utah received so many calls asking who was singing the song, they did a story on me. Which then turned into a media tour of all the radio and news stations over six months. The lyrics of the song were printed on billboards. And Coca-Cola used the song in their movie theater commercials nationwide. I had friends in NYC send me videos of the song playing in the commercials before they watched their movie in the theater. What a thrill it was.

I knew very little about sync at this time. It felt like a phenomenon, and I didn't understand how to repeat the process. So many things had to align for this amazing success. This was the first breadcrumb that I followed. I was learning how to step forward and take ownership of the way I showed up in my music and career. It took me a few more years to understand how to reverse engineer this success for more songs, placements, and other indie artists. We hope to help shorten that timeline for you with this book.

For more resources to help you land your first placement, please visit our website at 2Indie.com.

HOW MUSIC GETS PLACED

Each form of media tends to have a different process through which music is licensed. Below you'll learn the general path a song takes to being licensed, as well as the types of professionals you might meet along the way.

In basic terms, music licensing involves stakeholders, decision-makers, and artists.

Stakeholders are the production companies, organizations, brands, teams, or individuals that pay for a media project to happen. They are the folks in control of the purse strings, and therefore yield a massive amount of influence on anything they finance.

Decision-Makers are the professionals who decide what music could be used in a media project. In film and TV, music supervisors are charged with presenting song options to the director or showrunner, who has the final say in which songs will get picked for specific cues.

In the ad world, the advertising client or brand is the one who has the final say on the creative. Before the client's final say, there is a ladder of approvals that needs to happen. Typically that ladder starts with the day-to-day creatives overseeing the project, it is then routed to their bosses, the group creative officer(s) (CCO). Once there is alignment on all those fronts, the agency will send the creative option to the client for their final stamp of approval.

And of course, the **Artists** are the creators who provide the music! Music placed in media can either have been previously written and recorded, or custom-made for the specific project (this is commonly referred to as "bespoke" compositions).

Typically, the stakeholders hire the decision-makers to fulfill the music needs of a given media project. Then the decision makers, with a creative vision, budget and a deadline to adhere to, go out and find music from artists that they can legally clear for use in the project.

Here's a case study of how this journey can unfold.

Stakeholder - A major movie studio.

Decision Makers - The studio hires a director to create an original film. The director then hires a music supervisor to help fulfill the sonic side of their creative vision within the budgetary parameters dictated by the studio.

Artists - The music supervisor finds and clears music from various music artists for the project.

WHY NOT GO DIRECT?

Now you might be thinking, "Okay, great! So why not send my music directly to the stakeholders, cut out the people in the middle?"

Because there's an established process, sending your music directly to an international brand does nothing when that brand has already vetted and hired professionals that they trust (and have legally binding agreements with) to discover the perfect soundtracks for their upcoming media campaigns.

"Alright, so how do I send my music to the people who are contracted to make the decisions?" This is where things seem a lot simpler than they are.

Billions of licensing dollars are at stake each year across the industry. Who do you think the people are who *everyone* wants to build a direct relationship with? Yeah, that's right, it's the decision-makers.

Decision-makers, like music supervisors, often receive dozens, if not hundreds, of music pitches a *day*. These pitches come in from major labels and music production houses as well as from indie labels, composers, and artists. How can you cut through the noise? It's perhaps the biggest uphill battle in sync.

HOW SYNC AGENCIES CAN HELP

More and more indie artists are competing for attention and success in music licensing, so it's important to gain as much of an advantage as you can.

We believe *most* indie artists are best served by enlisting professionals to help pitch their music to decision-makers in sync. This is one of the ways you can gain that advantage: the power of agency representation. We strongly encourage you from our own experiences, to work with sync agencies to gain the upper hand.

Sync agencies are companies that pitch music to decision-makers in sync. These agencies (or individual agents) represent a catalog of songs they've curated from different artists that they have signed to their roster. In exchange for pitching music and handling the admin on any deals that come through, sync agencies take a cut of the licensing fees that come in from placements.

Perhaps the biggest reason decision-makers (such as music supervisors) love working with sync agencies is because they know they can trust them. Once they build a track record of successful song clearances together, it becomes easy for both parties to continue building upon that mutually beneficial relationship by choosing to work with each other on future projects.

Part of what this trust-building looks like is that agencies thoroughly vet the music they rep for any sample uses or other potential rights issues. So decision makers can trust that the music sent to them by sync agencies can legally be cleared without any problems. You are in pretty bad shape when a song has been cut to a scene and is slated to air on TV, and the network finds out there is an issue with the clearance of the song and the song might need to be pulled last minute. Yikes! To avoid situations like these, music supes prefer to work with sync agencies.

Sync agencies also vet music for quality and potential market demand. Their artists and repertoire (A&R) process for onboarding new artists to their roster ensures that the music they can deliver to decision-makers consistently sounds radio-ready. Decision-makers love knowing where they can conveniently find this level of high-quality music!

Another big advantage agencies have over indie artists pitching themselves directly, is experience. Agencies know the clearance game backward and forward. They are not going to ask a bunch of newbie questions about the sync process to a music supervisor, who doesn't have the time or interest in teaching someone about it. They know how to negotiate sync fees and help make the song clearance process as smooth as possible. It's key to have all of that on your side.

Also when a decision-maker sends a reputable agency a brief (a request for a specific kind of music for a media project), the agency is only going to send music that's highly relevant back to them. When the project needs indie rock, they aren't going to get synth-pop instead from an indie artist desperate to send something in for *every* opportunity out of the hope of finding a new audience for their music.

Agencies have strong personal and business relationships with decision-makers and commit a lot of time to nurturing them. They continually invest in expanding their quality network in the industry by attending conferences, going out to lunches, sending out gifts and cards, and connecting over the phone or Zoom. In all honesty, this is not stuff most indie artists have the time and resources to do on top of making music, playing shows, and engaging fans over social media, etc.

Agencies have many advantages over indie artists attempting to pitch themselves for sync. Yet pitching existing music to decision-makers and responding to briefs are only part of what agencies do to serve the sync industry.

Decision-makers often reach out to reputable agencies looking for custom pieces of music for their projects. These bespoke opportunities may then be forwarded to artists and composers on the agency roster based on who the agency feels is best suited for the job. Sometimes you'll get a demo fee for attempting to fulfill the brief, though many are offered simply on spec with payment coming only if you land the placement. Typically, you won't get briefs for custom work from an agency until you've proven you can create radio-ready music to order and do it quickly.

Another great thing that agencies can do for artists is match them for collaboration opportunities with other artists, songwriters, composers, and producers on their roster. It can be helpful to expand your creative network by working with other quality music makers in sync. This matchmaking frequently comes with the caveat that the agency will permanently take a cut of the publishing for any work created through the new collaboration... The positive to this is that the agency will then be even more incentivized to pitch the songs that are made.

SYNC AGENCIES LOVE HELPING ARTISTS

Check out what these professionals at agencies had to say about what they love most about their job:

"Although I derive much excitement at seeing/hearing an artist track in a placement we secured, the most fulfilling part of our work is when the syncs we land for artists are quite literally the difference between them continuing to follow their passion (making a living and life from music) or having it take a back seat to a more (immediate) financially secure endeavor."

Mike Soens, Founder
Lo Fi Music

"I love film, I love music, I love working with filmmakers who love music, but I also love helping artists feed themselves and pay their bills. So if I can help someone put food on the table, that's exciting to me."

Kristina Benson, Owner
Sweet On Top

"My favorite part of the job is finding trendy tracks and the hidden gems from CD Baby's vast and diverse catalog and landing DIY musicians a sync in a hit TV show, movie, or advertisement. The gratitude from artists when they get a sync, and real money, is awesome! Most of my placements are an artist's first! With millions of tracks at my disposal, I am always looking to stay on top of trends as well as find tracks that you would not traditionally think of as 'syncable.' CD Baby lands placements from trendy to the niche."

Brett Byrd, Manager, Sync Licensing
CD Baby

"My favorite part of the job is telling artists when a Quote Request or license has come through. I love to hear their excitement. That never gets old."

Kari Kimmel, Owner
Glow Music Group

"My favorite part of the job is helping artists not only earn money with their music but also pitch their music to Pepsi, Disney, A24, CBS Sports, and more."

Farnell Newton, Streaming & Distribution Specialist + Label Services
Marmoset

"I love to be able to connect both artists and music supervisors to the correct avenues to fulfill their creative endeavors in conjunction with the rest of my team here at Heavy Hitters Music. Assisting people to make their dreams come true is rewarding. Hearing stories of how we were able to find new music a home, or land a placement makes my job worth every moment."

Sierra Jordan, Sync Licensing and Administration Coordinator Heavy Hitters

"Empty Bar Gravitas"

When I was working for Catch The Moon Music (CTM), one of the things that was always on the table for me was to sign and pitch music that I loved and believed in. We would do weekly Zoom listening sessions where I would give feedback on music submitted by all the artists in the community who were learning how to license their songs. It was in early December 2019 when I was running one of these listening sessions and I heard "Gold" by Emily Anderson. I'd usually skip through songs as I would evaluate them on the spot, but this one grabbed me instantly and never let go. I played the whole song through and it moved me to literal tears on stream. After hearing it, I instantly offered to Emily for CTM to pitch the song.

Fast forward a couple of months and we were right in the middle of the 2020 pandemic. A big-time ad agency hit us up with a request. Miller Lite was looking for instrumentals for a national ad promoting awareness of a program they created to help bartenders across the country who had lost their jobs overnight due to the nationwide lockdowns. It needed to have "Empty Bar Gravitas." I sent them a playlist of songs, and I included "Gold" because I knew that the haunting but hopeful piano chords that started the song could be a perfect fit for something like this.

We quickly got bad news, that the spot looked like it was moving forward without music at all! Which was a heartbreaker to us, as well as our contact at the ad agency who is such a huge advocate for indie artists. That's always part of the game, the needs for a spot can change in an instant. The client was worried that music would distract people from the important message they were trying to deliver with the ad. The one bright spot was that "Gold" was chosen as the song they'd use if they decided it needed music. But that seemed unlikely.

Two days later, we got the amazing news that Miller Lite changed their mind, and that "Gold" would be the song used for the ad. It was a great payday for Emily. She was so excited. It was her first sync, so it was special for me to tell her. Quickly after she released the song and the campaign aired, the song would go on to rack up tens of thousands of plays and Shazams resulting in *many new fans of her music. This is my favorite pitching story from my time at CTM. It demonstrates how every license that goes through is a little miracle involving many people.*

For more resources to help you understand how agencies work and how they can benefit you, please visit 2Indie.com.

It should be obvious by now that the professionals who run sync agencies are huge fans of music, gigantic advocates for indie artists, and love nothing more than to get a win for the hard-working and talented music makers they proudly represent.

HOW TO GET SIGNED

Now that you understand what a sync agency can do for you, you can see the power of rep in music licensing. So how do you land a rep deal with a quality agency so they can begin pitching your songs? Let's dive in.

DIAL IN YOUR SOUND

One surefire way to get a rep deal is by doing the thing that's arguably also going to cause you to have the most success in landing licenses... By making ear-catching, broadcast quality music in modern genres that is actively needed for sync!

One common misperception that a lot of indie artists have when coming into the process of sync, is that they believe their back catalog of music is perfect for use in ads, TV, and film. That they are sitting on a "gold mine" with their hard drive. If your music can honestly fit seamlessly into a playlist of professionally recorded songs used in recent media projects, then your back catalog might be great for sync. Chances are, however, that your music is likely missing some of the things that would put it in high demand.

Here are the top 10 characteristics that successful vocal songs include:

- A compelling vocal performance
- A memorable vocal and instrumental melodies
- A focused lyrical theme that works for licensing
- Creative lyrics that fit the genre perfectly
- High production quality appropriate to the genre
- Strongly contrasting dynamic levels between sections
- Edit points in the arrangement (that make use easy)
- An arrangement that masterfully guides the listener on a journey
- A balanced mix and professional sounding master
- Creative artist branding that helps sell the song

The more of these things that are present in your music, the more desirable it will be.

"I would have to say that it's gotten more crowded with new sync companies and the overload of streaming music. It's impossible to navigate through all the artists that upload daily. This is a marked difference in today's licensing world."

Steve Scharf, President
Steven Scharf Entertainment

"With every passing year, this industry becomes more saturated. There are so many great bands and so much great music, it's difficult to stand out from the rest. I truly believe, however, that if you have great music that is unique - and work harder than everyone else - you can rise above the noise and be heard."

Kari Kimmel, Owner
Glow Music Group

Undoubtedly, the competition in sync has grown fierce. One question you'll want to ask yourself often is, "How can I make my music stand out?"

If your music sounds modern that can help. While having an authentic retro sound can be a great niche for sync, vintage niches won't present you with as many opportunities as those targeting modern genres. That's simply because there isn't as much ongoing demand for niche music.

It's important to say that if you find yourself artistically stuck in a past era, it may be your best bet to fully embrace that. Instead of trying to change your sound, be *the* source for authentic 1980s hair metal that's easy to clear. Being the best at a small niche that you are naturally good at and becoming well known for that in sync is a way you can "stand out," see results, and long-term creative fulfillment in licensing.

No matter if you make Hot 100 music or are sticking to the oldies, the best way to get started with finding a market for what you do in sync is by researching what's being used right now.

Here's a good list of places to start your online research:

- Tunefind - Extensive index of TV shows and their soundtracks
- TheMovieBox - For film trailers and TV promos
- iSpot.TV - For researching what's happening in ads
- Spotify - Many TV shows, films, games and other media have official soundtrack playlists that are easy to find

You can sometimes successfully use the Shazam app to identify the music being used in a piece of media. You can then track the artist down on Spotify and social media to start following them and learning from their sonic approach and branding.

Trends in sync are changing all the time, and it can be beneficial if the music you make is in line with what's currently hot. Keep in mind that if a trend catches on, you are instantly in competition with all the best custom composer/writer teams in the world who are 24/7 gunning for syncs. So if you're late to the game, it might be best to instead think of what might be catching on next.

"The important thing about a trend (aside from being aware of it) is sensing whether it is likely to be a long-term trend or a short one. Eras are walls built from trends, so knowing which bricks will define the era will keep you relevant."

Drew Sherrod, Creative Director
Ghostwriter Music

An important step in research is finding a couple of reference songs that you like that work for sync and that you could envision yourself making similar music to. Music that would seamlessly fit into a playlist with the references. It only takes one reference song to get started. You can use tools like Spotify song radio to algorithmically generate a playlist of similar songs. And voila, you have chosen a modern genre and sound that works for music licensing.

Then it's just a matter of executing on creating your new music. In short, you'll need to professionally write, produce, mix, and master the songs. Then when you're done, create a compelling branding package to support your pitch to rep agencies.

Assuming you have the musical goods ready to pitch, let's talk now about what you can do to maximize your chances of making a good impression with sync agencies. This process of getting repped starts with finding quality agencies to pitch your music to.

For community and accountability in dialing in your sound so that it works better for sync, consider joining our private licensing club called The Sync Society. You can find out all about it at 2Indie.com/SyncSociety

FINDING QUALITY SYNC AGENCIES

While the contact info for key decision-makers in music supervision and advertising can be nearly impossible to find, quality sync agencies can be easy to find with online research. Here are a few steps you can take to research agencies and see what kind of placements they are getting and what kind of artists they represent. We highly recommend creating a spreadsheet to track each of the agencies you are researching.

- Lean on the homework others have done before you. Google "Sync Agencies" or "Music Licensing Agencies." Compile the lists you find into one big list. This will be a great starting point.
- Take your list and look each agency up on social media platforms. You'll find a lot of agencies post their recent placements and releases from artists on their rosters. Which agencies speak to you the most?

- Check out each agency's website, paying close attention to how recent their placements are, how big their artist roster seems to be, and what kind of creative vibe they are giving off. Many agency websites will also have a page featuring their team so you can get a feel for who is working at the company.
- Most sync agencies often have a presence on LinkedIn. This can help you learn more about the people who work at the agencies.
- Once you gather some names associated with each agency, try searching for them on YouTube. Are there interviews or conference panels featuring them? This can be a great way to start to get to know the personality of someone you might soon be reaching out to.
- Also definitely go back through once you have names of people at specific agencies and look them up on social media. Many of the people who work for successful sync agencies have an active online presence themselves.
- Artists can also be a great source when it comes to agency research as well. Often when an artist gets a placement they will give a shout-out to the agency that pitched their music for it. Following similar artists in your genre that are landing placements can help you learn about agencies that are finding traction with music like yours.

Let's keep gathering info on sync agencies and work towards the best possible professional matches. As you continue down the rabbit hole with each agency, add columns to your spreadsheet:

- Do they have recent placements?
- What types of music do they represent?
- Does their website state they accept unsolicited submissions?
- How do they accept submissions? Is there a contact email or submission form?
- Do they seem to focus more on TV and films, or ads?
- Do they represent artists that seem similar to you?
- Does their roster have mostly indie artists or artists signed to labels?
- If it matters to you, how does their culture make you feel? Do they seem to reflect your values/champion causes you believe in?
- Do they seem to have a gap in their roster? Might they be on the lookout for marketable music similar to yours that they don't already have?

On how agencies find new artists to work with...

"I tell people who want to work in showbiz that it is more than a job. It is a life. The answer to this is a good example. I never 'go looking' because I am always looking... So I may hear about talent in a conversation and then follow it up. I have gone down the rabbit hole on YouTube and found things. I have tried to make group deals with labels that I love and ended up with a couple of bands that opened for some of the artists on said labels. And I have been curious about some weird-looking so-and-so on LinkedIn who I figured would be either amazing or on the waiting list for a mental hospital. I suppose some people have reliable sources, but I have always found that reliable sources aren't reliable for the next cool thing as much as more of what you already like... WHICH IS GREAT... but you can't be a master chef if you're cooking with someone else's recipes."

Drew Sherrod, Creative Director
Ghostwriter Music

BIG NAME AGENCIES VS. SMALLER COMPANIES

There's no shortage of options in terms of different agencies and agents to choose from to rep your music. The big-name agencies are going to have higher-profile artists attached to them, and perhaps a steadier stream of lucrative placements with major brands, networks, and studios. There are pros and cons to working with a big name agency:

- Pros:
  - You can say you are repped by the big name agency and that alone may give you clout in some circles
  - They may have access to more lucrative licensing opportunities because of their track record and artist roster
  - They can usually offer you worldwide publishing admin (sub-publishing) so you're collecting

everything you can from any placements that come through

- A reputable sub-publisher can collect all of the international royalties that you will not otherwise collect through your PRO (Performing Rights Organization), which can amount to pocket change or a fortune depending on how much the projects your songs are used on are viewed worldwide

- Cons:

  - Often deals with big name agencies are more restrictive and they may take a bigger cut of your sync fees
  - You can easily get lost as a small fish in a sea of higher profile artists
  - You may not get as many opportunities because they are focused on fewer, more lucrative projects

Smaller sync agencies can be a great fit for indie artists, but there are pros and cons with them as well:

- Pros:

  - They may have a smaller roster so you have less competition for their time and attention to your music

- They may have more time to help develop your sound in sync and facilitate collaborations
- They might have a steady pipeline of smaller opportunities since their business model isn't as dependent upon landing highly lucrative placements

- Cons:

  - They may not have the level of professional connections required to be in the loop on more lucrative placement opportunities
  - Especially with individual pitch agents, they may be way in over their head in having to run an entire operation on their own
  - They might be "song collectors" who honestly aren't really landing any placements in spite of putting out the public appearance that they are an active agency

Now that you have an understanding about agencies, it's time to start thinking of how you can get creative about approaching them: What are your ins? Do they accept unsolicited submissions? Potential in roads include:

- Do I know any of their employees?
- Do I know any artists that are repped by them?
- Do I know any songwriters or producers that have worked with artists on their roster?

- Do they have recent placements on shows, films, and ads that use music similar to the music I make?
- Do I have music that fits in with what they already have on their artist roster?
- Do I offer something unique that could complement their artist roster?
- Do I have anything in common with the people who work for the company?
- Do I champion the same causes the company appears to?
- Have employees of theirs recently said anything publicly that I learned from, was entertained by, or related to a lot?

Using the answers you've collected so far, start to rank the agencies based on how good a fit they might be for you. Prepare a list of 3-5 agencies to start.

For our free list of 100 sync agencies that you can start doing your research on immediately, visit: SyncAgencies.com

MAKING YOUR BEST CASE FOR REP

Before reaching out, it's important to spend some time making the best case for yourself. Put together a compelling branding package that includes:

- Words

    - Elevator Pitch: Imagine you have 10-15 seconds to tell someone the who, what, where, and why of your music. Try to limit it to 20 words if you can, and work on it until it feels natural to say and easy to use in a conversation. Practice it on friends and acquaintances and keep tweaking until it's right.

    - Artist Bio: This expands upon your elevator pitch, providing more depth to your story.

    - Press Quotes / Soundbites: If you have compelling press quotes, that's great! If you don't, then have a couple of friendly artists, songwriters or producers write you quotes that reinforce your brand.

- Sounds

  o 3-5 Songs: Your best work only. It helps if all the songs feel like they fit on a playlist with each other and accurately represent the music described in your elevator pitch and bio.

- Visuals

  o Artist Photos
  o Album / EP / Single Cover Artwork
  o Music Videos / Live Performance Videos. Optional, but agencies love to work with artists who are releasing songs, dropping videos, and playing shows in person to support their art.

Using the branding assets you've assembled, create an EPK (Electronic Press Kit) using a platform like DISCO. DISCO has a feature called Pages which makes it easy to place all of your marketing materials onto one easy-to-share page. While there are other EPK platforms out there, DISCO has become the industry standard in sync so we recommend using it. If you don't have a DISCO account yet, you can get one here and save: SaveOnDISCO.com

Learning to Pitch

When I started working in sync at Catch the Moon Music, I had no idea how to write a pitch email. I probably used to do all the things I now coach my clients not to do. Which is to say, I wrote my whole life story, included all my credits, included a bunch of links for them to do the work of clicking around and trying to figure out who I was, what I had to offer, and maybe even attached an mp3 instead of a streamable link. Oh snoooooze!

If I received an email like that today, I'd just pass it right on by. Not because I don't care, but because I don't have the time to figure out what you're trying to share about yourself and how we can work together. If you are pitching someone, let them know clearly what you do, what you sound like, and why you are reaching out.

I may not have known how to write a great pitch, but I was eager to learn and jumped right in. I was lucky to learn from the best, founder of Catch the Moon Music, Cathy Heller. For the first month of working for her, we would dissect each pitch email I sent and practice cold calls in her kitchen. I remember one day she took out two jars of peanut butter and asked me to pitch them to her on the spot, as if I was cold-calling her. I did. And she gave me pointers and then I tried again. We went back *and forth like this. This is where I cut my teeth in pitch emails and cold calls.*

I learned how to infuse a pitch email with personality, specifics, and connection. I learned that a pitch is about creating a lasting and personal relationship with a real human, and it starts with being real...and succinct.

The results speak for themselves. I landed placements for the artists we represented. I created relationships with sync agencies, music supervisors, and advertising agencies I still have today. And I'll tell you why.

1. *I had something that was of value to them (great, easy-to-clear music)*
2. *I was personable. I took the time to get to know each person, learned what they needed, and let them know about me.*
3. *I followed up. People are busy, emails are missed, and following up is such a gift when done respectfully and warmly. Often people are grateful for a follow-up. I know I am.*

When we can understand the person on the other side of the pitch is human just like us, we can connect and partner in substantial ways.

HOW TO PITCH YOUR MUSIC TO SYNC AGENCIES

Now that you have done your homework, you are ready to pitch. Just keep in mind that pitching is often a protracted process that requires patience and business savvy. We recommend starting with no more than 3-5 agencies you might like to have rep your music. If they have a submission form on their website, then fill that out. Most of the time though, you will be reaching out directly to a sync agency through email. So we're going to cover the keys to making your best pitch via that format.

EMAIL STRATEGIES

Keep your pitch short and to the point. People can read about 30 words in 15 seconds. So if you keep your email under 60 words, the recipient can read the entire thing in 30 seconds. Try to limit your initial email to 60 words. Don't worry, there's a lot you can say in 60 or so words!

Be friendly. Honestly complimenting an agency or the specific employee you're reaching out to can be a great way to help break the ice. Just make sure it's brief, you want to mainly spend your words making the case for your music being a potential match for their roster.

Be sincere. It is important to be genuine and truthful in your pitch because it establishes a foundation of trust and credibility. Allow them to get to know the *actual* you. A big part of respecting people's time is not approaching them with a fake attitude or other kinds of bullshit. So be real when you reach out.

"Professionalism! I love it when an artist knows the business, has checked out our site before submitting, responds to emails quickly and concisely, has clear and documented agreements with co-writers, and of course, makes top-quality music. In short, someone who's easy to work with. To be honest, our top earning artists are people we don't hear from a whole lot — they're busy making music and have found a way to streamline everything else."

Dan Waldkirch, Vice President of Operations and A&R Crucial Music

Consider who you are and who you are reaching out to. Some people are less formal than others in their interactions. Use what you know of them and their company's ethos to design your approach. For example, if your music is edgy, then it might be a good idea to pitch to people and companies with a slight bite or attitude to the way they do business, making your email less formal... While staying true to yourself, adjust your strategy to the specific person you are reaching out to.

"When an artist/songwriter pitches a song or two to me, I like to know they have done their homework. In other words, they have looked at the website to see how they should pitch a song and are pitching directly to me rather than a blast to several people. I would like to know how they learned about Song And Film. I also like to see some metadata embedded in the track or the email. Some artists/writers go as far as to tell me more about themselves and the songs they are pitching to me which is great!"

Glory Reinstein, President
Song & Film LLC

Use your elevator pitch. A lot of the time, if you just copy/paste your elevator pitch (that you've finely honed) it will do the perfect job of introducing them to both your personality and music.

"Of course it's great when artists have their instrumentals and vocals in the same link, and when they clearly communicate clearance info. But it's becoming more and more important that the artist has a clear artist identity that they can talk about. Are they playing shows? When are they releasing music? Do they have a label? Also, do they have a sync history? That kind of information can set an artist apart from the rest."

Kristina Benson, Owner
Sweet On Top

Test your streamable EPK link. No matter what platform you've used to create your EPK, and triple-check to make sure the link you are sending them works. Use an incognito window in your web browser so you can be sure your link doesn't require a login anywhere in order to work.

On attachments and links when pitching for sync...

"I don't mind an attachment if it is unbelievably rare, or if the circumstance makes it appropriate. For example, I had the perfect song for an urgent request, but it was an old song in an archive on Dropbox. The person requesting was NOT a fan of Dropbox (or Box or anything that isn't DISCO), but I sent it anyway with a note saying I know it's not the way they want it, but in light of the situation, I hope they would give me a pass, just this once. It worked. Dead links are just annoying... but much more annoying if they're from someone you don't know or has made the mistake before."

Drew Sherrod, Creative Director
Ghostwriter Music

Subject line. Try to include genre-specific info in the subject line in an eye-catching way. You can copy/paste from your elevator pitch here too. If someone is introducing you to the agency, you could use the subject line to say "_____ told me to reach out to you about rep"

NO CC or BCC. We cannot emphasize this enough! Copy/paste pitches are easy to spot, and nothing is going to get your email deleted faster than someone seeing they are part of a large blanket email. It's annoying to get blasted like this, no matter how well-intentioned it is. It can be especially bad if you CC a bunch of people on the same email and they can all see each other's addresses. Super unprofessional.

It's fine to use a template when pitching, but take the time to customize the template so that it feels personal to each person you send it to. And send each email out separately.

Use email tracking. You'll want to make sure you're using some kind of email software that enables you to track when someone opens an email you send them. This will give you peace of mind that your emails are being delivered and yield valuable info for subsequent follow-ups.

There's no perfect pitch template that exists for every artist in every situation. But it's hard to go wrong with this simple format:

- Short salutation - "Hey _____, hope you're having a great day."
- How you learned about them - "My producer _____ told me about your agency and I had to look you up."
- Your elevator pitch

- Stating your desire for a professional rep - "I'm looking for a sync rep for my music."
- Inviting them to check out your EPK
- "Thank you for your time." or "No rush on reply."
- Closing with "Best, _____" or whatever you prefer here

Don't Take It Personally, Keep Taking Action...

Before I started working at a music licensing company, I had no idea how busy an agency could be. I had no idea how many hats a sync agent wears, or how hard it is to reply to every email. I had no idea how many emails went unanswered, not for lack of caring but for lack of time.

I quickly learned that when you don't hear back from a sync agency right away, it is NOT personal.

I wanted to take a few minutes to break down just a few of the hats we wear when running a music licensing company.

The many hats of a sync agent ...

Pulling Songs Hat: Filling the incoming briefs from supes and agencies each day. Each day, multiple times a day, a sync agent receives an email with a search/brief from a music supe or ad agency looking for a certain type of song for a project they are working on. A sync agent then goes through their catalog pulling songs that might fit the lyrical theme, genre, and budget requirements of the search. If you get a handful of these a day, your day could be filled.

New Music Hat: Listening to new music being pitched. An agency's inbox is always full of new music being pitched for rep. So if there is downtime, an agency will try to go through the emails and listen. The last thing you want to do is miss an amazing artist or song.

Artist Paperwork Hat: Onboarding new artist material and negotiating contracts. Every time you find a new artist you want to sign, you have to negotiate the contract, answer questions, go back and forth for a bit, make any agreed-upon changes, and then onboard the music into your system. Onboarding looks different for every agency, but the basic idea is that you need to know:

- How to clear the song... Is it one-stop, is it not one-stop, and is there a publishing company involved?
- Who owns writers, publishing, and master shares of the song?
- What are the keywords contained in the lyrics?

Then you have to onboard the lyrics and tag the song with relevant genre information and lyrical themes.

Pitching and Networking Hat: Sending outbound emails to existing contacts and making new ones. To support the artists you represent, it is important to stay top of mind for music sups and ad agencies. This means sending emails with purpose, meeting for coffee and lunch, traveling to meet new contacts, and finding creative and meaningful ways to connect with new music supes and agencies.

Landing a License Hat: Negotiating and papering the deals for all licenses. When a quote or a license comes into an agency from a music supe or ad agency, the agency is responsible for papering the deal. They need to fill out the paperwork, sometimes that means getting the okay from the artist (depending on the deal of the agency), making sure the budget is correct, the ownership parties are correct, etc.

Artists are Happy Hat: Managing artists on the roster. When you represent a roster of artists, they check in regularly with you. They want to know what trends you are seeing, what you might need, if you can send a pitch report, and why they haven't received their payment. Or they send you new songs to upload in your system, etc. It is important to stay connected to the artists you represent and hear what is new in their music lives as well.

Money Hat: Tracking invoices, payments, and paying artists. After all that, the agency must keep track of payments sent or not sent, follow up on delinquent *payments (this happens often) and once payment is received, pay out the artist and the agency.*

So the next time you wonder what might be happening over at the agency or feel like a lack of response might be personal, consider all the hats they are wearing and how you best can help support them as a great team player. Drop them a timely follow-up or check-in.

"Everyone you email is human, and we like to receive things our own way. Do your research! I like concise emails that let the music speak. I love artist stories and how they got into music, their influences, etc., but start with a hello and a streaming link. I want the emotion and story of the song to hit me first and then I'll read on further.

Please don't over-hype yourself. Confidence is important for any artist, but if you say you're the next Grammy award-winning artist or compare yourself to one, then your music had better live up to that!

It's also a huge plus to call out some artists we already work with and/or some placements we have achieved for artists on our roster. It makes your email feel real, rather than a mass mail-out. You have to do the work to find out who you are emailing, as we do (and still have to be on top of) with our clients. Making a database of contacts is the easy part."

Will Chadwick, Senior Sync Creative
A&G Sync Music

20 Seconds Of Courage

"20 seconds of courage." A phrase I first heard from Cathy Heller, the most impactful mentor in my life. Although my career in sync started before I met Cathy, it was not until I met her that I began to learn how to reverse engineer the process and go on to land hundreds of placements for myself and other indie artists.

When I first started running the boutique music licensing company Catch The Moon Music, part of my job was to research advertising agencies and cold call 25 agencies a day, to create new contacts for our catalog of indie artists and be a resource for the ad agencies.

Cold calling and cold emailing takes a certain type of courage I hadn't called on so consistently before. The more I did it, the more I built up my courage muscle.

I would hype myself up before each call, ready to connect with the other person on the line, make a memorable *impression, and create a new real relationship of trust and sync success.*

Sometimes people were too busy to bother being kind or receptive to my call. And a few times someone was pretty rude—I can still remember the names of the two rude people. It was hard to brush that off in the beginning. But mostly people were grateful to learn about a new one-stop catalog and have a real conversation with someone they could work with.

One day I hyped myself up to call a new ad agency I had heard a lot about. Someone answered. We ended up having a 20-minute conversation that started somewhere around music and moved to our geographical locations, favorite vacation spots, and parenting advice. My new friend then forwarded my contact information along with a sampler playlist of music from the catalog to all the producers at the agency. Two weeks later I received an email from one of the producers asking if I could pull any upbeat songs about friendship. Umm, heck yes! We had a lot of those in the catalog! I sent over a playlist right away, all one-stop. There were about three rounds of back and forth between us where they asked for a few more musical idea options. And in the end, we won the spot. It was a well-known brand that paid the indie artist a good sum. That is the power of courage.

Through my cold calls, I set up live performances for myself and the artists I represented in the ad agency offices. I flew to New York and Chicago for meetings with music supervisors and ad agencies and worked with some of the top agencies and music makers in the biz. Not because I am the best, but because I have had courage...most of the time.

20 seconds of courage translates to all places in our lives. The hard conversations we need to have. The email, pitching our music to the sync agency of our dreams. Showing up in a new community of music makers and putting our music out there for feedback. When we push ourselves outside of our comfort zone to achieve the life we desire, we build a greater aptitude for courage, and it opens a world of opportunities each day.

For more resources, community, and accountability for pitching your music to agencies, consider joining our private sync club The Sync Society by visiting 2Indie. com/SyncSociety

TIME TO PRESS SEND

Pressing send can be the scariest part of the entire pitch process. Not to worry though, you've done your research, made your best case for rep, and you're only going to get the feedback you need if you put yourself out there. Once you make that initial pitch to 3-5 agencies, give them some time to respond to you.

If you get "no" for an answer, don't sweat it. Remember, nothing in the music business is personal. You've got a long list of agencies to pitch to so it's just time to go to the next on the list.

Follow-ups are smart when pitching your music to agencies. Sometimes someone just doesn't see your email at all, or receiving a polite nudge simply reminds them to respond. Just make sure to keep your follow-ups friendly, and brief, and don't send one too soon. Wait at least two weeks after your initial pitch.

REASONS AN AGENCY MAY PASS ON YOU

So they pass on pitching your music. Remember, even if it truly hurts sometimes, it doesn't help to take it personally in the music business. No matter how you feel about it, there are perfectly valid business reasons an agency may decide to pass on your pitch:

- Your music needs improvement in the form of better songwriting and production
- Your music may sound great, but just isn't in high demand in sync
- Your music is in a genre they don't work in
- You work in a genre they already have too many signed artists in. Agencies don't want to "cannibalize" their roster by signing you.
- You need more development as an artist (bigger fanbase) so you can bring more branding leverage into sync

Remember, it's not their job to tell you how to improve your music or even why they passed on your pitch. It's not even their job to respond to the pitch at all. If you've pitched your songs, and even sent a polite follow-up, and gotten no response chances are they simply are passing on your music. Oftentimes when agencies write to inform you they are passing on your music, they will just say something simple, polite, and nondescript. Sometimes they'll be super cool and supportive when breaking the news. Always take the high road, even if you are disappointed with an agency's decision. You may have new (and improved) songs to pitch them soon, so it's best to keep the door cracked for that possibility.

No Slam Dunk

In late 2016, I finished my first EP of what I considered to be quality music to pitch to sync agencies. I had planned all along to find a reputable agency to rep it. I had narrowed down a short list of 3-5 agencies and started with my first choice. I had the producer I was working with send the pitch because they had a solid relationship already established with the agency. A week goes by and there's no response. I was anxious and still optimistic. I thought my music was a perfect match for the kinds of opportunities the agency frequently pitched for.

Then the day came when I got a short message from the producer saying something like, "Sorry, we'll talk in the morning." They forwarded me the email they had gotten, and I took these words from the agency personally: "I don't love it. I like parts of it but it doesn't feel like a slam dunk for me."

I was disappointed. My top option turned me down. What could I do about it? Nothing. The songs were done, and I still needed to find a rep for them. I had to put my personal feelings aside and go down the list to options 2 and 3. So that's what I did. I pitched Music Alternatives directly, and they seemed genuinely interested. I had a sit-down meeting with the owner of the company, and I got a really good vibe from them. The deal I was offered seemed fair and the contract looked well written. I signed with them, and like 3 months later I landed the international Starbucks spot that changed my entire music career as well as a placement of another song on Hawaii Five-O on CBS.

I printed out the rejection email I had gotten and kept it pinned up at my studio where I would see it every day. It was a great reminder that in sync you should always keep working to improve, while also fighting hard to get your music represented well. It was also a way for me to remember that the journey you go on may look very different from what you envision being the best possible path. Even though I was massively disappointed at one point, in hindsight it feels like I was truly guided to the right agency all along!

RESPONDING TO INTEREST FROM AN AGENCY

When you get a response from an agency indicating they'd be interested in your music, it's the perfect time to connect with them more closely. If you live in the same geographic area, grabbing a coffee or lunch is ideal. If you live far apart, we recommend hopping on a Zoom with them. It's the next best thing because you get some visual feedback through Zoom that you don't get on a phone call.

Why not just sign a deal over email? Well, the reason we don't recommend it is that the music industry is truly a relationship-based business. So many placements happen because of a personal connection between the artists and their rep, and the rep and their contacts in the supervision world. You ideally want a sync agency that honestly loves what you do and is going to go to bat for your songs. Otherwise what can happen is your music just sits on a hard drive somewhere while being locked into a deal that may prevent you from doing something else with it. The best way to read what kind of relationship you're going to have with an agency is by directly talking to the people who are going to be pitching your music. Insist on a meeting.

SYNC AGENCY MEETING TIPS

During your meeting with a prospective sync rep, here are the kinds of questions you will want to ask them:

Are they Exclusive or Non-Exclusive?

One of the questions we get asked the most is if it's better to be in a non-exclusive sync rep deal or an exclusive one. Non-exclusive rep means that while the agency you sign the deal with pitches your music, you are also free to pitch it directly, and you are even able to sign non-exclusive rep deals with other agencies as well to assist in pitching. Exclusive rep means that the agency you sign the deal with has the *sole right* to pitch your music for sync. No one else can pitch your music. It's a highly committed relationship from a legal standpoint.

So which is better? Although there are pros and cons to each, we recommend finding an exclusive rep for your music if you can. One reason exclusive rep can be better is that many decision-makers in sync (like music supervisors) are very sensitive to multiple people pitching them the same song. Some may even blacklist you if they see your song coming to them from more than one place. This is because they may have been burned in the past with disputes between agencies pitching a song they use. They don't want to deal with any potential situation where your song is perfect for the placement, and then they don't know who to clear the song with. It's just easier for them to look for other options that they know they won't have a potential problem with. Another reason exclusive rep can be better is that when someone commits exclusively to pitching your music, they have more skin in the game because they know they are the only ones who can deliver your song to the sync market.

Just remember, you don't have to commit ALL of your songs to one exclusive deal. You can mix it up if you want. Very few sync agencies out there require you to commit all of your songs exclusively to them. Diversifying your "rep portfolio" can be a good thing. So you can potentially have an album repped exclusively by one agency, and then save another project or batch of singles for non-exclusive rep by a couple of agencies. Mix and match as you like, as long as it all makes sense and feels right for your long-term strategy.

WHAT ARE THE MAIN DEAL POINTS?

Let's talk now about the other important legal points contained in a sync deal.

Clearance Authorization - Will you approve every sync before the agency agrees to it? Or does the agency have the legal ability to authorize clearance of your music without your involvement at all? Some deals insist on getting your approval of all potential placements as they are developing, while others you may only find out about a placement well after it airs.

Splits - What percentage of master sync fees does the company take when they land you a placement? Master sync fees are the up-front fees that are paid out from a license agreement. Typically you'll see anywhere from 25% to 50% as the amount an agency takes out from master syncs before they pass the rest on to you.

An often overlooked aspect when it comes to master syncs and agencies is the "All In." When master syncs are paid out, half the money is owed to the master owners of the recording itself, and the other half is owed to the publishers of the song. Those halves combined constitute the "All In." Some agency deals only take their cut of master syncs from the master side, while others take their cut from the "All In" before passing the rest onto you.

Term - How long is the rep deal in effect? The shortest deals we see are month to month with a 30-day cancellation notice, and some go as long as... forever! That's right, if you see "in perpetuity" in your agreement, this means that your songs are likely locked into the deal at least until you die. Maybe until the sun blows up billions of years from now. Now *that's* commitment. Most deals tend to fall into a 1-3 year term range with automatic yearly renewal if neither side terminates.

Termination - How can either party end the deal? Most rep deals have automatic renewal clauses, but provide a window (typically 30 to 90 days long) where either side can terminate the business relationship when the term ends before that renewal triggers. Some deals simply allow either party to terminate the deal at any time.

Payouts - How are sync payouts to the artist handled? Some agencies pay within 30 days of receiving payment for a license, while others pay out quarterly or after hitting a certain payout threshold.

Pub Admin - Does the agency offer publishing admin for its artists? Agencies may require the artists who have signed with them to enter into a publishing admin deal with them (also known as a sub-publishing arrangement). This allows them to take a cut of the backend royalties generated from TV, streaming, and other sources that are collected by performance rights organizations (PROs) like ASCAP, BMI, SESAC, etc. It's a way for them to have more "investment" in your songs should they succeed in sync. Other agencies make it optional to utilize their publishing admin, or simply don't offer that at all.

If you are considering opting into publishing admin with an agency, make sure to ask if the term for the publishing admin deal is the same as the sync rep deal. If you eventually terminate your deal, it would be ideal to be able to also opt out of the publishing admin deal at the same time so you can regain full control of your pub when you go back out to market shopping for a new deal for your music.

Retitling - As part of a deal, a non-exclusive agency may insist upon retitling your songs. When you agree to this, the agency re-registers your songs with a PRO using a unique title that makes it possible for them to only collect royalties from public uses of the song in media that they have secured the placements for. Just be aware that there are some potential pitfalls of opting into retitling. For example, some non-exclusive agencies simply refuse to rep songs that have been retitled. Depending on who you ask in the industry, retitling can either be considered completely fine or a total dealbreaker. So if retitling is a deal point, make sure to fully research the pros and cons so you can make the best-informed decision for yourself.

WHAT'S THEIR PITCH PLAN?

What kind of briefs would they pitch your music for? Do they have ideas of specific decision makers (like music supervisors) to send your songs to? Do they regularly curate and send out industry samplers that your songs will be included in? If an agency has a plan for pitching your music and can put it into words, that is an indication they will be eager and ready to take productive action should you sign a deal with them.

"SONG COLLECTORS"

Beware that there are some disreputable sync agencies who seem to make it their mission to just gobble up as much easy-to-clear music as they can. They aggressively add artists and their songs to their catalog as fast as possible, often with a lower quality standard, perhaps in the hope that if they become a gigantic warehouse of music they'll be more likely to be able to serve requests no matter what they are and who they are from. This is a form of putting the cart before the horse, as often these agencies don't have a consistent track record of success or the staffing power to leverage a large catalog of songs. They are "Song Collectors". You don't want to be added to someone's collection. Your in-person meeting with an agency is the perfect time to determine how serious an agency they are, what their recent track record is, if they have a solid game plan for pitching your music, and if your music will be given the attention and consideration it deserves if you join their roster.

DO THEY FACILITATE COLLABORATION?

Teaming up with like-minded creatives can lead to tracks that really slap for sync. Does the agency connect artists with other artists, songwriters, and producers on their roster for collabs? And if so, would they be looking to do that with you? What does that process entail, and what extra cut does the agency take with songs created under these circumstances? It's common for agencies to take a cut of the publishing in these scenarios — in perpetuity.

HOW DO THEY FULFILL BESPOKE / CUSTOM OPPORTUNITIES?

Agencies often field requests looking for custom pieces of music. When this happens, agencies will reach out to their most trusted composers and artists on the roster to create the perfect track for the brief as fast as possible. These types of jobs are often, but not always, done on spec. This means you won't get paid anything unless the track lands the job, and you may be in competition with others on the roster for the gig. Sometimes a demo fee is paid whether the song lands the placement or not. If you're a self-sufficient composer or an artist with a fast production team, it can be great to be plugged into an agency's pipeline of bespoke opportunities. Ask about how custom requests are handled by the agency and if you may be considered for such jobs.

For incredible insights each year as to what sync agencies need, how they work and what you can do to impress them, visit 2Indie.com for more resources. Or email us at way@2indie.com and we can point you to the correct resources for you.

Almost Never

If you build great relationships with your collaborators, and your skills complement each other well, you may find yourself on the receiving end of invites to work on random bespoke projects. In the summer of 2019, my friend Dario Forzato hit me up with an opportunity he was given through 411 Music Group, an agency I had long admired, but never had a direct relationship with myself. The idea was to make teen pop songs for a show on the BBC, and the most exciting part about it was that if we landed the gig the show cast members would professionally record and perform our music. All live on TV!

It's interesting with Dario. He had been introduced to me by a close friend in 2015 as someone I could connect with about learning to produce. I still didn't even know what a compressor did back then! I paid him several times (by the hour) to come to my studio and teach me some tricks in ProTools. Then I hired him to help out on some productions of mine that I was struggling with, and over the course of working together over the years we became friends. Dario is an amazing composer, but not really a vocalist. So it makes sense that he would perhaps ask me to work with him on some vocal songs for this BBC pitch.

The crazy thing about this opportunity is that we had to make 3 songs for it within a week. I honestly had no idea whether or not I could help write music that teen girls would love. Or find a great female singer who was perfect for the demos and also available to track on short notice. But Dario asked me if I could do it, and I just confidently said, "Yes."

So what did we do then? On Monday, Dario and I sat down for 90 minutes and wrote the choruses to three songs with the instrumentals he had prepared. Then I needed to find the singer and write the rest of all three of the songs before Sunday. There were a couple of singers I reached out to that I would have loved to work on the songs with, but none of them were available. The week was flying by and I still didn't have a singer lined up. Ut oh. Then I remembered my buddy Sam Knaak was telling me about this singer Kimi Lundy Liope (artist name King Klio) who he had worked with on some pop stuff. She had been on my radar for quite some time. So with my fingers crossed, I hit her up and by some miracle she not only was down to do it, but she was also available to track vocals with me on Friday night and Saturday.

Sure we had never worked together before, and I had no idea what her voice would sound like on these... But I had faith we could get it done.

So Kimi rolled in on Friday night at 8 PM and we wrote the rest of the songs, and also tracked the main vocals for all of them. In five hours. We were having such a fun time. We hit it off instantly. We went back in on Saturday to do stacks, harmonies, and ad-libs. Then I sent the edited and tuned files off to Dario, he mixed them in and sent the tracks off to 411 well in time. A couple weeks later, one of the songs landed, and the artist Girls Here First released our song "I'm In Trouble" in 2020 after recording and performing the show live on the BBC in season 2 of the hit show Almost Never.

I think this story goes to show that a lot of amazing things in sync can happen when you build good relationships, say, "Yes!" when you get the opportunity, and do everything you can to over-deliver when you get that chance.

Do They Provide Pitch Reports?

Whether your songs are landing placements or not, it can be helpful to know the types of opportunities your songs are being pitched for and how frequently that's happening. Some agencies proactively create pitch reports for the artists on their roster and make them available, while others do it upon request.

Artist Support

Indie artists can use all the help they can get when it comes to marketing their releases. Does the agency you're talking to help support artist releases in their email newsletters and on social media? The social media channels of sync agencies can almost look like that of a record label. Artist release announcements, sync placement alerts, behind-the-scenes vignettes, artist takeovers, etc. Can your upcoming artist releases be included in these marketing efforts?

WHAT IS A "GOOD SYNC DEAL"?

So after all of these points are considered, you're left with the question of whether the deal being presented to you is a good one or not. This is a bit of a controversial subject, because honestly everyone's assessment of an agency and the deal they offer (fair or not) is partly determined by if they land you any syncs.

As far as any rep contract goes, the three biggest things you may wrestle with are whether they are exclusive or non-exclusive, the percentage they take from syncs, and the length of the deal.

Consider an extremely "artist-friendly" deal: it's non-exclusive, they give you 75% of all master sync fees, and you can cancel at any time. Then consider the opposite: you are exclusive with them, they *take* 60% of all syncs, and you are locked in for 5 years.

On the surface, it seems like a no-brainer which deal you should sign... right? The truth is, either of these deals could be awesome or terrible. This is because <u>nothing</u> in sync is guaranteed. We would argue that on paper the "artist-friendly" deal is worse since there's almost no commitment on either side, and the agency has almost no incentive to aggressively pitch your music.

The real test of a deal is what the agency will do with your music in the valuable time you are giving them to commercially exploit it. Remember, modern songs do not age like fine wine! They are going to have a shelf life of maximum desirability in the market before they become less popular or even niche.

Sometimes the whole decision becomes a gut check. How do you feel about the agency's excitement level about signing your music? Does it feel like they are going to go to bat for you, or is it likely you will sit on a hard drive somewhere throughout the deal with little to no ongoing conversation between you and the agency?

"Our agreement is already very friendly to artists compared to others out there, so I generally don't allow people to negotiate. If there's an artist that is filling a gap in my catalog I might be more flexible. I'm running the business solo,

> and I'm also getting a lot more high-quality music submissions than I can handle, so it's not in my best interest to make special carve-outs for any particular artist."
>
> Elaine Ryan, Founder
> Unicorn Sync

The truth is that a deal that appears unfriendly to the artist on paper can be very lucrative for both sides. Getting back to those theoretical deals presented earlier, 75% of nothing is way worse than 40% of multiple placements. Giving all your tracks to one agency can be a lot better than giving your songs to five different agencies and having nothing happen with them. A deal that's offered is rarely bad strictly based on the terms. What happens after the deal is in place and they are working for you that counts

One of the most important things to understand clearly before you sign is how to get out of the deal if you decide it's not working out. Do you understand the term and any termination stipulations you need to abide by if you want out of the deal?

Ultimately, signing a rep deal should be an exciting thing celebrated by both parties. As with any new business relationship, the parties need to trust each other and build on that trust over time as true partners in licensing.

Don't Forget A "Vibe Check"

Vibe check time. How do you feel after talking to the agency directly? Is anything unclear after asking these questions? Don't be afraid to ask. Remember, you want to sign a rep deal with an agency where you can both be excellent business partners with each other. Rushing that process is unnecessary. And not fully understanding what you're getting into is a music career self-sabotage.

If both parties feel great about working together and wish to proceed, then you'll be presented with a legally binding sync rep agreement.

NEGOTIATING YOUR SYNC REP DEAL

In the excitement of signing a deal and getting rep for your music, one thing can get overlooked: it may be possible to change some of your deal points with an agency. For example, they may be willing to work with you non-exclusively instead of the usual exclusive deal they offer. You might be able to skip opting into their publishing admin. Or they may be willing to bring down the length of the deal from three years to two.

Your ability to alter the deal offered to you will hinge upon a couple of things. First off, how much does the agency see a real demand for your music? If you have clout as an artist, that can help. Also being able to skilfully articulate why you want to change the deal can help you convince them to make a change. Just be aware that the rep deal being offered to you may be the only deal that the agency offers to everyone on their roster.

INVOLVING A LAWYER

Most sync agency rep deals have a lot of similarities, but there's no contract template that everyone uses. Whenever you're signing a legally binding agreement it's important that you completely understand what it is you're agreeing to. This is where hiring a music attorney can be incredibly helpful. Many lawyers in the music industry offer friendly rates to indie artists for simple things like reviewing a rep agreement. Before you consult an attorney, ask the agency all of the questions you have about the agreement. Agencies are accustomed to answering questions about their deals, and they might be able to clarify a simple matter to your satisfaction without needing to involve a lawyer.

IT ALWAYS FALLS BACK ON YOU

One thing that's important to understand in the sync business is that honesty and transparency about your music are mandatory. If you lie to an agency about copyrighted samples that you used, or about your sub-publishing deal, it's always going to fall back on you if the song gets entangled in a legal dispute. Being a professional means understanding everything about the music you make, and describing it accurately in terms of all of the songwriting and master rights. If you enter into business honestly, you won't run into problems.

"I don't care if artists aren't one-stop but I do prefer for a supervisor to be reaching out to an actual publisher, label, or sync licensing agency instead of an unrepresented writer. An experienced or competent manager with a reputable management group can work as well. Also, be careful about using (royalty-free sample libraries such as) Splice and then claiming with a straight face that your song has no samples. Particularly if you're using vocal hooks that you've taken from Splice. Don't forget: Splice is a sample."

Kristina Benson, Owner
Sweet On Top

THINKING IT OVER

Once you've been offered a rep deal by an agency, it can be tempting to sign it right away. It's better to think it over carefully. There are reasons for this beyond just making sure you understand the agreement and feeling like it's a great professional match. You may have pitched the same songs to a different agency and are waiting to hear back from them. In this case, it's fine to just say something to the effect of, "Thank you so much, I'm going to review this agreement, and I'll get back to you as soon as possible on it." As other agencies are being pitched other songs all the time by other artists, they can assume that they might not be the only agency you are talking to. Honestly, most agencies are too busy day to day to worry about whether you're going to sign the deal they've offered you. Don't leave them hanging to dry on this though. If you have a deal on the table, respond to it as soon as it's reasonably possible.

Whatever you do, don't sign a deal out of fear that you won't be offered one by anyone else. Think of actually signing a rep deal with an agency as another "vibe check." It's okay to meet with an agency, get their agreement sent to your inbox, and then walk away from the offer. You need to do what is in your best interest in the music industry, and sometimes saying "no" is exactly what needs to happen for you to take the next step forward in your career.

SIGNING YOUR DEAL

Nowadays you're almost always going to sign your rep deal using an online signature (e-signature) solution like Dochub or Docusign. Just because physical ink doesn't touch any paper, it doesn't make your legal document any less legally binding, so definitely take anything you put your name and signature to in this fashion seriously.

We'll now start to talk about the things you'll want to do to maximize your chances of thriving in your newly minted sync rep deal.

When you are considering agencies or negotiating your deal, if we can be of help on your journey let us know. You can email us at way@2indie.com.

WHAT HAPPENS NEXT?

So now that you've taken that big step of entering into a rep deal with an agency, what's next? Let's break all of that down now.

AGENCY ONBOARDING PROCESS

After the digital ink has dried, your new deal begins in earnest with the onboarding process. Each agency has a different way of doing things and a different amount of support staff. Depending on their specific needs and their ability to help hold your hand throughout the process, it's going to result in more or less work for you to get officially brought on board the roster.

It's important to follow through with the onboarding process as quickly as you can, because your agency likely will not pitch your music at all until the process is complete. Some of this work can seem incredibly tedious to creative types, but power through it. Complete honesty and thoroughness is key when it comes to the information you provide to your agency during onboarding. Nothing is going to derail trust faster than your agency finding out that you weren't honest about your publisher splits when you onboarded because it has caused a real snag with a song clearance.

SCHEDULE A

If it wasn't completely spelled out in your initial agreement, the entire list of songs that the agency is going to pitch on your behalf will be completely defined in what's called a "Schedule A." This is a list of all the songs that will fall under the terms of your rep agreement. Only include songs in your Schedule A that you want in the deal. We don't recommend randomly adding back catalog songs that you haven't explicitly discussed a pitching strategy with the agency. Unless you just want them to collect your songs for no reason?

METADATA

Now it's time to address another matter that has little to do with creativity but has everything to do with you getting paid as a creative. When your songs are recorded, and the final files are delivered, you'll end up with high-quality sound files such as .WAVs or .AIFFs. Aside from the name of the file itself (like "good_song.WAV", the DAW that created it doesn't usually pre-encode anything else to distinguish it from any other sound file out there. This is where you step in and provide the metadata — the key information to encode into your files so that when someone opens them up, they give instant confirmation of who created and owns the music, how to contact them, and other details that help a sync professional easily use your music.

The simplest way to make sure you have all of your bases covered is to get a DISCO account and use that to upload and manage your sound files. DISCO provides metadata fields that are clearly labeled and easy to fill out. We recommend using the "Comments" field to include your full contact information, song splits, as well as relevant keywords to describe your music. DISCO can even generate these keywords for you in a surprisingly accurate fashion through a feature called auto-tagging.

> "Metadata is usually very important, but can also be an area of much drama, depending on how many people/companies have represented a song. If the metadata is clean and makes sense, then great! If it is inconsistent and confusing, it usually means the song (and/or agency) is too. I think of metadata sort of like a car's interior. If it looks cared for, the car/ driver probably is too."
>
> Drew Sherrod, Creative Director
> Ghostwriter Music

There are folks out there who sell courses about music metadata, making ridiculous claims that if you don't fill out your metadata a certain way you will lose out on opportunities. Rest assured that this is not the case, and don't spend money learning about metadata. As long as you cover the basics, and always make sure your current contact information is easy to find in the "Comments" section, someone will always be able to find you if they have questions about your music.

One important thing to note, .MP3 and .AIFF files can carry metadata, while .WAV files cannot. That's why we recommend using .AIFF for all of your high-resolution master files.

Every agency you work with is going to have a slightly different way they prefer to handle metadata. Most of them have their own system of doing it so that they have a uniform approach across their entire catalog. They may have you encode your metadata for them in a specific way before you send it over, or they may just have you provide all of your metadata in a spreadsheet template so they can easily do it exactly the way they prefer. Always a good idea to have a spreadsheet of all of your metadata for this reason.

YOUR FILES

Let's talk more about the actual files you will typically be sending a rep agency after you sign a deal with them. These are the files you are going to want to have handy:

High Res Masters: These are your stereo .AIFF files at a sample rate of at least 48 kHz and a bit depth of at least 24 bits. The 24/48 combo is commonplace in broadcast and works for most applications.

MP3: When you make your MP3 files, we recommend 320kbps for high sound quality.

Instrumental Mix: Always include instrumentals of your songs.

Clean Mix: If your song has profanity, provide a clean mix whenever possible.

TV/Performance Mix: This is a mix of your song without the lead vocals on it. Artists will use these mixes to perform when they don't have a band supporting them. The mixes can also come in handy for sync purposes. It's common to hear songs with just the background vocals and "oohs" placed to picture.

Stems: These are the grouped stereo files of a song that when put together constitute the entire song mix. Most times these are separated by group into lead vocals, drums, bass, keys, guitars, percussion, and background vocals. It's incredibly useful to have these handy for every song in your library. Especially in advertising, being able to create a custom mix of a song allows for so many more creative possibilities vs. just one stereo file that's already mixed. Being asked for stems is a very positive sign that your song is being tested to picture for a placement, and if you can't deliver them fast upon request, it's unlikely your song will be in contention for long. Things in sync can move quickly and when a decision maker (like a music supervisor) can't get what they need from your song for whatever reason, they are always thinking of five other options available to replace it. So definitely get stems for all of your songs. Some agencies require stems when you onboard, though most understand that it's going to be tough in some situations to get them. One option that AI has made possible is the algorithmic creation of stems from a stereo file. There are already several solutions that allow you to input your stereo file and get generated stems from them. They are not going to be the same quality as creating stems from your DAW (or tape) source, but if you have no other options they can work.

CONTACT INFO

How will the agency contact you? Make sure they *always* have your current contact info on file. This is especially important if you change your email or phone number, as your agency may reach out to you with urgent requests such as authorizing the response to a TV show quote.

TAX & PAYMENT INFO

Many agencies will onboard you into their payment system whether you have gotten a placement or not. In the United States, this will involve you sending them a signed W-9 form so they have all of your tax information to report any payouts to the IRS. And then they may have you register your bank information with them for direct deposit, or simply get the handle for one of your online payment accounts like PayPal or Zelle.

If you find yourself overwhelmed by getting all your "ducks in a row" for sync, let us know if we can help along your journey. You can email us at way@2indie.com.

HOW THE ARTIST/ AGENCY RELATIONSHIP TYPICALLY GOES

Now that we've broken down the sync agency onboarding process, we can cover the basics of what the typical artist/ agency relationship looks like in terms of what they'll be doing for you, what the clearance process looks like, and how to keep a realistic perspective on it all.

THE DAY-IN / DAY-OUT OF WHAT SYNC AGENCIES DO

Every sync agency has professional contacts with different decision-makers in licensing. These may include music supervisors, supervision companies, ad agencies, trailer houses, etc. So the day in / day out of any agency is going to vary, sometimes wildly. That said, the basic business strategy agencies employ is:

- Fielding requests (briefs) from their licensing partners
- Sending out specific playlists to fulfill those requests
- Following through on the clearance process with their licensing partners (and you) to see any placements through
- Paying out anyone who is owed money after the placement happens

When an agency isn't actively working on pitches and clearance, they may be:

- Marketing their business and artist roster through samplers and social media
- Providing client services to their roster (such as facilitating collaborations)
- Considering new music to add to their catalog (A&R)
- Administering their catalog
- Managing their payout system

Larger agencies may have one person or even a team assigned to any one of these business activities. Keep in mind that if you are working with an individual agent, they may be handling everything mentioned above by themself. So that's an important thing to keep in mind when you are corresponding with an agency. You want to politely reach out to the right person to address the matter, and also have a realistic mindset around their capacity to quickly respond to your inquiry.

UNDERSTANDING THE CLEARANCE PROCESS

Aside from the creative process of picking the perfect song to support a story being told on screen, clearance is the most important process to understand about sync.

In general, clearance entails securing all of the rights necessary to legally synchronize a song to a media project. There are many types of media clearances, but for simplicity's sake (and because most of the placements that indie artists typically secure are going to fall under this) we're going to focus on explaining the song clearance processes for TV, film, and advertising.

THE CLEARANCE PROCESS FOR TV & FILM

The clearance process for TV and film are similar, so we'll use TV as an example. When a music supervisor of a TV show has been pitched your song by an agency and decides they might like to use it for a cue in an episode, the next thing they do is send what is called a quote request to the agency that pitched them the song. This document specifies how the song may be used in the show, and how much the production company is offering to pay to license it. At this point, your agency may reach out to okay the request with you. Once the quote request is negotiated and approved, then there's a short (or long) waiting game to see if your song is actually used in the show. A couple of song options might be pre-approved via quote requests for the same cue. If your song is chosen for the show cue, then a final licensing agreement will be sent over to your agency to be signed by the agency that is acting on your behalf. This legally binding document finalizes the clearance process so that the production company has all the rights they need to air the scene your music is used in.

THE CLEARANCE PROCESS FOR ADVERTISING

The clearance process for advertising is similar to TV and Film in that the rights to the song in question need to be cleared to use with picture. If an advertising agency is working on the commercial, typically the business affairs team will work hand-in-hand with the legal department. If the ad agency has a music department, all three of these teams work together to make sure all the rights are cleared for the song. That means contacting the sync agent and /or publisher that represents the song. Once the client of the advertisement gives the final yes to the song selection, a Master Recording and Music Composition License is sent to the sync agency and/or publisher. This form includes all the project info, term, licensing fee, timing of the song, exclusivity details, and media use.

Now that you understand the basics of the clearance process in TV, film, and ads, it's time to talk about how to handle assumptions you might have as your agency begins pitching your music.

If you have further questions about the clearance process, feel free to email us at way@2indie.com and we will do our best to get you answers and connect you to the right resources.

THINGS YOU SHOULD AND SHOULDN'T ASSUME

In a healthy business relationship with a sync agency that is repping your music, there are assumptions you'll want to make, and ones you'll also want to avoid like the plague.

Assume:

- Your songs are being pitched for relevant opportunities in sync by your agency *when they are the best options in the catalog* to be included as a response to a request they receive
- Your agency negotiates the most competitive fees available for a placement of one of your songs
- You will be paid as soon as the agency gets paid under the terms of the rep deal you signed

Don't Assume:

- Your agency isn't pitching your music when you haven't gotten a placement yet (or in awhile)

- Your agency isn't pushing hard enough and should ask for more money on your behalf when you are presented with a quote request - often for indie artists, sync fees are more or less set in stone based on available budget and pushing for more in these cases is just going to take you out of contention for a sync

- Your agency is intentionally delaying payment to you for a placement - it can take a long time for your agency to get paid for a placement of one of your songs (network TV master sync fees can sometimes take over six months to be paid out to your agency)

HOW TO TRULY THRIVE IN YOUR SYNC DEAL

Let's now talk about going above and beyond with the agency that reps you. These are the things that are going to help put you in the upper echelon of your roster, regardless of the demand for your music.

THERE ARE NO GUARANTEES IN SYNC

Remember that no matter how hard your agency is working for you, there are no guarantees in sync. Sometimes you might have great music for licensing, but the right opportunity just never lands in the inbox of your agency for them to pitch it. Or you could just lose a spot to another great song. That happens all the time.

The important thing is to make sure you aren't taking any loaded expectations into the deal you make with your agency. If you have an entitled attitude towards the people who are trying to help you out, it doesn't make them more of an advocate of yours.

BE PATIENT IN SYNC

It's rare for an artist who signs a sync rep deal to find instant success with landing placements. The first obstacle is that it takes time for agencies to fully onboard an artist. The onboarding process itself can take months. Then it takes time for an agency to effectively market the music of a new artist on their roster to their sync contacts. Some agencies are aggressive with industry samplers and meetings with decision makers on new artists on their roster, while other smaller agencies and individual agents may mostly be responding to briefs and sending songs out only when they are the best fit for those opportunities. Since it takes time no matter which agency you sign to, we recommend being patient with the agency you have trusted to pitch your music.

RESPOND PROMPTLY TO SYNC REQUESTS

If your agency reaches out to you asking for ASAP approval of $4K all-in to clear a song for background use in a popular show, now isn't the time to let that email sit in your inbox while you get your workout in. Drop what you're doing and just let them know if you can do it or not. They need to let the music supervisor know ASAP and the supervisor likely has multiple alternate song options ready to go if they can't clear your song quickly. Some deadlines are super tight, and your fast response to requests is always appreciated — and remembered.

HAVE A "YES" ATTITUDE IN LICENSING

Going back to that $4K all-in, are you the type to agree to those terms, or are you going to give them a lot of pushback? One way to get yourself in the doghouse quickly is by building a reputation as someone who is going to make a clearance difficult. Understand that in most cases, the amount being offered for your song is the most the show has budgeted for. Indie artists don't typically have the kind of pull to succeed in hardballing negotiations anyway. That's why it's best to have a "yes" attitude when building a relationship with your new agency. They ask you for stems? "Yes, I'll get those over ASAP." Can you be flexible by taking what appears to be a low master sync fee? "Yes, thank you!" This kind of attitude is remembered by all parties involved. It can also be rewarding. Who do you think they are going to think of first the next time they have a more lucrative opp in front of them? It's the folks on their roster who make clearances both a breeze and a pleasure.

GO WITH THE FLOW OF AN AGENCY'S TEAM

In larger agencies, the business organization structure and the people involved can change rapidly. Team members in an agency can change often, so don't be shocked if you suddenly get an auto-responder from the person who signed your music to the roster saying they have left the company. Not to worry, losing your champion doesn't have to be a death sentence to your prospects of a fruitful relationship with an agency. If you find out your contact at an agency has changed roles or is working elsewhere, politely ask whoever you can at the company who your new point person is. We recommend asking for a meeting with your new contact so you can introduce yourself and begin building rapport with them. Relationships are the most important thing in the music industry, and you don't want your music in a place where no one is thinking of you and going to bat for your songs. So go with the flow when changes happen at the agency that reps you, make a professional attempt to establish rapport with new employees, and then you can act accordingly to serve the interests you have with them.

REGULARLY FEED YOUR AGENCY NEW SONGS

Don't be like the person at the open mic who comes back every week to belt out the exact same song wondering why they get the same response every time. If you initially signed an EP with your agency, what's the next song or batch of songs you are planning to deliver to them? Even if it's quarterly, giving your agency new music of yours to pitch keeps your brand and sound in their mind, and demonstrates to them that you are an active artist which shows and brands prefer to partner with. Think of sending new songs to your agency as a wise investment of sorts with potential big payoffs further down the line.

REGULARLY RELEASE MUSIC YOURSELF

More on the subject of being an active artist... Are you releasing enough music? Almost without exception, the hottest indie artists in sync make regular public releases of their music. It's part feeding the algorithm, part continuing to reinforce your brand, and, honestly, shouldn't that be part of the proactive fulfillment of your artist journey anyways? Artist releases are a great excuse to reach out to your agency and enthuse them even more about pitching your songs. Brands and networks love adding active artists to their projects because there's more potential for cross-promotion and organic engagement when there's a "real artist" with a following involved. You don't have a following yet? Well, let's just say you're not going to start getting one by sitting on your songs! Better to get the music out there regularly, for sure.

REGULAR COMMUNICATION WITH SYNC AGENCY A&R

Once you get into a flow with things, it's a good idea to stay in touch with your agency A&R at least every quarter to get a feel for what new music is needed by the agency. It can help you decide what new records to make, and the A&R can help you brainstorm potential collaborations to meet the active needs of the agency. Keep in mind that not every agency has a dedicated A&R, but every agency has someone you can have this type of conversation with, even if it's the single agent who runs the entire operation.

If you need private coaching on how to maintain amazing relationships with the sync agencies that represent your music, it's something we specialize in. We would be glad to help you out. Please reach out to us at: way@2indie.com.

HOW TO UNDERSTAND A SYNC BRIEF

When you're signed to an agency, you may be put onto their brief distribution email list. Not all agencies do this. Some prefer to keep their searches close to the vest, while others like to involve parts or all of their artist roster in meeting the immediate needs of their clients.

If you do start getting briefs, it can be a real game-changer. It will help you understand what the week-in / week-out needs of an agency can look like. As well as inform the music you are making.

Let's first go into what briefs (also called "searches") tend to contain. Keep in mind, that these are our categories. In the real world, briefs may just contain a paragraph of informally written copy. Although many of these categories do end up as points on a final licensing agreement:

1. Media Project Description: This is where you'll get a general feel for what they are looking for. You'll find out if it's for an ad, TV show, film, video game, etc. They may even tell you the brand or network it's for. Sometimes they'll go into some detail about what's happening visually, occasionally you may also get a rough cut of the ad or scene. Some briefs are going to be super specific about what they need and give very narrow confines to the search, while others are going to be more general.

2. Reference Songs and/or Artists: This is one of the most important pieces of information that a brief may contain, as it can give you a clearer idea of what the client wants. Sometimes they are looking more for a specific kind of sound that a particular song has, while other times they are more looking for music that fits seamlessly into a playlist with the songs they reference. Often, you'll be given specific instructions on how to interpret the references. For example, they may say they like the aggressive guitars on one song, and the soft synth pads on another that help to glue it all together. Or they may need 1970s disco like such-and-such band.

3. License Fee: They may tell you up front how much the sync pays if it lands. You'll want to look for "ALL IN" here. Often, the quoted amount will be for clearing both the master and publishing sides. If it's

not "ALL IN," then the quoted amount will be for the master and publishing sides separately. In other words, a bigger potential payday. If it doesn't pay a lot, often agencies will let you know that ahead of time so you can have realistic expectations.

4. Use: They may tell you exactly how the song is going to be used in the project, and the specific length of music needed.

5. Term: This is how long the license is for. This is going to vary wildly depending upon the type of media and the amount of commitment the client wants to have to use your song. For example, TV promos may be for only a single day, while most indie films tend to ask for rights in perpetuity... that's right, forever!

6. Exclusivity: What kind of exclusivity is the client asking for with a potential license? Some deals are exclusive across all media and industries. Others are much more flexible. In an ad, they may only exclude you from licensing your song with a competitor in their industry for the duration of the license, for example. This would still allow you potentially to license your song to another project at the same time as long as it's in a different industry. Or it might be exclusive to a form of media such as streaming or broadcast television, allowing you to still license the song to another media format such as podcasts or video games.

7. Territory: Where does the license apply? If it's a worldwide license, then you are giving the client worldwide rights to use the song in the formats agreed to in any agreement. A lot of times you'll see a license apply only to specific countries. It may even only apply to your metro area or state/province.

PROFESSIONAL ETIQUETTE FOR BRIEFS

If you receive briefs from your agency, here are a few basic ground rules you'll want to follow:

1. You are usually getting a redacted or rewritten brief from your agency that they got directly from a music supervisor or ad agency. It's okay to ask questions if something seems too vague. Just keep in mind that there are going to be briefs where the client isn't exactly sure what they want, so some leeway or room for creative interpretation may apply and your agency is just passing that along.

2. NEVER try to reach out directly to the people involved in the creation of the media project by hitting up the music supervisor, etc. Trying to circumvent your agency is about the most unprofessional way you could respond to them including you in a search. The sync community is extremely tight-knit, and

going behind people's backs is not something you want to be known for doing.

3. If they preface a brief by saying it's confidential and for you only, it means exactly that. It's not something for you to share freely with other people. Remember, the invaluable client relationship your agency has may be put into serious jeopardy if it should come up that you shared the brief with others.

4. If they do send you a link to the in-progress edit of an ad or scene, it's likely to be under a non-disclosure agreement (either verbal or written). Always err on the side of keeping things like this shared with you close to the vest. It's wise to ask for permission if you need to share any aspect of the project with collaborators, etc.

5. Only respond if you have something they need. The fear of missing out can be hard to resist, especially if it's a high-dollar placement. Understandable as that is, the only thing you're doing is potentially damaging the relationship you have with your agency by wasting their time. If you become someone known for carelessly responding to briefs, you may start to be ignored and might even be taken off their email list entirely.

6. Unless they say they want as many options as possible, don't send them more than your best 3-5

options. It's probably all the music they are going to reasonably have time to screen for the opportunity.

7. Don't expect a response from the agency when you respond to a brief... At all! Placements happen all the time when the agency doesn't have the time to respond to your email by saying "This works great, thank you!" This is because they are usually too busy to do that when they are concerned with sending the best songs they can to the client. You also aren't usually going to get feedback from the agency if your songs don't fit the search in their opinion. You want to avoid getting that kind of feedback, anyway for previously stated reasons.

CONTINUING TO EVOLVE YOUR SYNC SOUND

As you grow as an artist, songwriter, or producer in sync, you are going to find different opportunities to explore new genres and themes. And you may be doing it with completely new collaborators which can be exciting. Unless you've got your sound totally dialed in, it's best to keep an open mind about what you could do in sync.

Many established artists out there have sync side projects that land them lots of placements. They create different monikers so they don't have to tie the new music they are exploring with their established artist brand. With this approach you have the artistic freedom to do what feels authentic in your artist journey, while at the same time, you can always try a new sound out. And what you learn about writing "for sync," is honestly probably going to make you a better music maker overall. Better writing, production, and branding. Look for ways to keep evolving as the sync landscape changes, and you may just find yourself in the running for stuff.

"Over the last decade, the sync industry has grown exponentially in terms of the amount of licensors and artists vying for coveted spots. Keep the integrity of your writing, performance, and production top-notch to give yourself the best chance of success!"

Michael Fey
Shoot The Noise

A Song Licensed 8 Times

One of the most magical parts of sync for a music maker is that the same song can be licensed over and over again. When a song is licensed, that means you retain all the ownership of your song, and you can license it again and again. You never give up ownership. The exception is when you license a song to a brand, there usually is a term for which the song cannot be licensed to a similar brand for a period of time or when there is a buyout situation for the song.

I have gratefully experienced the magic of sync. I have two songs that have each been licensed eight or nine times and others that have been licensed five or six times. For example, one of my songs "It Makes Me Feel Good" has been synced nine times for spots like Del Lago Resort, four different Nivea ads, two Zynga ads, a Starbucks spot, and twice on Teen Mom. The moral of this story is, it is about the quality of the music, not just the quantity. You don't always know what song is going to be the one that is licensed over and over again, but you do know when you take the time to create a song that moves you, that you love, that is pro-quality, and that feels current with the needs of sync agencies, you are on your way. Great music creates opportunities for multiple placements while also retaining the ownership of your song.

"Great Big Day" Superfan

In March 2019, I popped open my email and found a strange-looking message from someone named "Wilmo" in the UK. He was a Poundland store employee, and one of my songs "Great Big Day" had been playing over the store speakers on repeat for months. The song was not released, but I think I maybe had the lyrics up somewhere publicly searchable. With some resourceful detective work, they somehow tracked the song back to me and found my email address. They wanted to know if I could send them a recording of the full song to listen to. How flattering! I just sent him back an MP3 of the song and he was so happy.

It took me a bit of work myself to figure out how the heck that song was playing in-store in the UK. I found out that a licensing company I had sent the song off to when I was first starting out had gotten it playlisted. It wasn't much money, but it was amazing to have someone from halfway across the globe reach out to me to find a cheery and catchy tune I'd made. This is just one of hundreds of interactions I've had with people around the world who found my music through licensing. This story is a good example of how passionate music fans can be, and why it's important to make sure to release as much of your finished music as possible so that people can Shazam it and easily find you.

BEING REPPED BY MULTIPLE SYNC AGENCIES

Finding just one agency you love and committing to an exclusive deal with them across your entire library of songs can be a great way to go. Oftentimes the more committed to one agency you are, the more likely it is that they are going to reciprocate by fully leveraging their resources on your behalf since they have more "skin in the game." This could include things like supporting your artist releases through sending out industry samplers or featuring the releases on their social media and website. They may be more enthused about pitching your music in general because they know they have a special business relationship with you that no one else has.

All of this said it can be fine to have your songs repped by a couple of different agencies. Spreading parts of your library around to different agencies can make a lot of sense, but we recommend having each of your songs repped by just one agency. Remember, if a decision maker is pitched the same song by two agencies, the confusion could have dire consequences. We've heard of some supervisors "blacklisting" artists who they receive music from through multiple agencies. Whether you are put on a permanent "naughty list" or not, it's best to have your songs repped by just one agency so that it's always crystal clear which agency reps your music.

One final thing we'll say regarding having your music repped by multiple agencies: it can be easier to network your library to music supervisors when you can just tell them your music can be cleared by one agency (vs. parts of your library here, other parts here, etc.). Picking one agency isn't what we necessarily recommend everyone do, but as you can see, the complicating factors can multiply the more agencies you work with at the same time.

WHEN YOUR AGENCY LANDS YOU A PLACEMENT

The first sync you get will surely be exciting news, no matter how big a cue or spot it is. Relish it and celebrate your first victory lap in the music licensing arena. Let's cover what you'll want to know when this magic moment happens.

You might find out about a placement from your agency in a few different ways. If it's a big one, they may call you directly to share the news. You may receive an email confirming that a license has gone through. Or you might hear from them well after the fact. In some cases, like if there's no master sync fee involved, you'll possibly learn about it from the cue sheet in your PRO's backend. With the frequently frantic (last-minute) nature of media production, agencies often don't know ahead of time whether your song was chosen or not for a project until it airs. This is fine because the terms will have been agreed upon previously, you just won't know about it until after it happens.

When you get a placement, make sure you let all of your collaborators know as soon as possible. But hold off on making big social media announcements until you are absolutely sure the placement is airing or has aired already. We can't stress this enough. Sync deals can fall through at any stage in the process. The best practice here is to wait until your placement airs, get a good recording of it if you can, and then make your big announcement then. Or do your push the week the show is about to air, if you know for sure that it's being used.

For TV and streaming, if a cue sheet is being filled out by the show's music supervisor, and they are asking your agency for all the pertinent details like artist name, song title, and splits...It means that the song was included in the episode since a cue sheet is only filed once they know for sure what the final finished product contains.

It could be worthwhile to ask your agency if they are planning to announce the placement on their social media. If you are planning to release the song to a Digital Service Provider (DSP) such as Spotify alongside when the sync airs, that could be another compelling reason for your agency to put you in the spotlight. The more clout you have as an artist, the more likely it is that they will do this sort of thing. But don't sweat it if they don't want to do it, some busy agencies land too many placements to even share about everything they secure for their clients each month.

If you did release the track through DSPs, did you make sure it's findable using Shazam? If you haven't done this yet, consider doing so ASAP. When a show airs with your music in it, people will often pull out their phones to find music that they like. It doesn't always happen, but sometimes artists blow up just by having one prominent placement and then everyone is wondering "Who's song is THAT!?" If your sync is on a prominent show and used memorably, then it's likely you'll see a good spike of Shazams... And hopefully, new streams and fans to go with it.

We encourage you to share all of your sync wins, no matter how big or small they are, with our public Facebook group called "Sync Friends - Music Licensing Community." If you aren't a member yet, please look us up or you can go directly to: https://www.facebook.com/groups/syncfriends

SPLITTING SYNC PROFITS WITH YOUR COLLABORATORS

When you contract with an agency to rep your music for sync, it's not unusual for you to become the "point person" for all of your songs included in the deal. This means you are viewed as a legally binding party who can 100% authorize all of the rights to all of your songs. Many sync rep deals don't require individual contracts with all the various writers, producers, and artists on your songs. As long as you legally agree that the songs can 100% be cleared, you're good to go. You will be seen as the point person for all the songs that the agency is repping of yours. So when payment for a placement comes in, they don't go tracking down all the master and publishing owners. They will typically just pay you directly for the full amount. When you get paid by an agency, it's part of your job to pay all of your collaborators their fair share of any master sync fees that come in. Do it in a timely fashion. Remember, the all in for a master sync comprises 50% master rights and 50% publishing rights. So you only take your share of each side and then distribute the rest according to the splits you agreed to with your collaborators when the songs were recorded.

For example, let's consider if you land a $100,000 master sync payment from an agency for a song use, and you own 100% of the master and 50% of the publishing of the song that was placed. In this case, you would take all of the master side ($50,000) and 50% of the publishing side ($25,000) meaning you would keep $75,000 and distribute the remaining $25,000 to the other publishing owners. If it's for a large amount, sometimes agencies will agree to distribute direct payouts to each of the rights holders. In the US, if you are paying people out from a check or wire transfer you receive from your agency, don't forget to 1099 them if the amount is over $600. You'll need to report these payouts to the IRS so you aren't held responsible for the tax liability on them.

EVALUATING YOUR CURRENT SYNC DEAL

There may come a time when you decide that an evaluation of your current sync rep deal (or deals) is wise. There are a few things you can do to make the best professional decision for yourself as an artist.

- Review the Deal: What are your options in terms of renewing or terminating the deal? Are there deadlines to be aware of in terms of giving notice before an auto-renew kicks in, or are you free to leave the deal at any time?
- Meeting with Agency: If you're feeling like you might like to switch agencies, it can be helpful to have a meeting with the agency that currently reps you to gauge their continued level of excitement in repping your music. You can also get a feel for how pitching your music is going, and for any upcoming opportunities the agency is involved in.

- Pitch Report: Anytime a year after signing with your agency, it's perfectly reasonable to request a pitch report. A pitch report outlines the times your music has been pitched. It often contains the dates, opportunities, and specific songs of yours that were pitched. This report will help you understand the activity level of the agency and how often they have included your songs in the pitches they have sent out.

Often having a meeting with your current agency will renew interest in both sides to continue working together.

ENDING YOUR SYNC DEAL

If you decide to end your rep deal, you will want to carefully follow any instructions given in the signed rep agreement you have with the agency. Some require written notification by a deadline, and sometimes that means you need to mail them a letter declaring your intention to withdraw from the deal. Though most deals can be ended now over email or perhaps a phone call followed up by an email.

Whatever you do, make sure that when you terminate the deal you receive a response from the agency. If they do not respond, follow up with them until you get a response because you'll need to know they received your request to end the deal. Even though it's fine to follow up aggressively on a request to terminate a deal, keep all of your communications polite. You never know, you may come back to them years later to work with them again. And as we mentioned earlier, agency teams change all the time and someone you're currently working at an agency you're

146 | Get Signed In Sync

dissatisfied with may suddenly become your point person at another agency you sign with. The music industry can be such a small world.

Your Music Matters

You never know who needs to hear your music and how deeply it may affect them. One of the wonders of having your music licensed is the exposure your music gets to so many people watching the show or commercial.

I have heartwarming stories of how my songs reached others who may never have heard my music if it were not for the license.

My song "You're So Good For Me" which was placed in a Coca-Cola and the amusement park commercial, touched people beyond my wildest dreams.

One day, I received an email from a mother in Utah. Her daughter was hospitalized with a coma, and she would only "wake" when my song "You're So Good For Me" was played on the commercial. It brought hope and light to the young girl and her family. A few news channels got wind of this story and reported on it on the daily news. I could hardly believe my song could make such an impact.

And it's not just about life-altering moments; it's about forging connections. A New York fashion designer slid into my Twitter DMs because my tune moved her. Next thing you know, we're sipping coffee in the Big Apple and a lifelong friendship born out of a licensing deal. Who'd have thought?

Most recently, a mom whose daughter was in the intensive burn unit at a hospital reached out to me to tell me my song was the only thing that made her little daughter smile, and how it brought joy to all the children there who were fighting for healing. It's not just about charts and numbers; it's about making a difference, bringing joy to kids fighting battles we can't even fathom.

Music licensing is not just a way to make money in music. It is a way to make a difference. It is making music that matters, helping tell stories with visual media, and having a chance to reach more people with your voice, words, and music.

It matters what you write. It matters that you care about what you create. It matters that you keep showing up for your dreams and your music. That you make the best music you can. Your music changes lives.

CONCLUSION

Whether you've read this book almost cover to cover, skimmed around a bit, or impatiently skipped straight to this final section...Thank you! We made this resource in the hope that all the indie artists, songwriters, and producers out there with quality music can use the knowledge and practical strategies contained within to make career-changing connections in sync. May you have great success in building the team you need in the music industry to make things happen for licensing your music.

We highly recommend you make as many friends in sync as you can. For most people, we've found it's more productive and a lot more fun to take the licensing journey together with other like-minded music makers. We warmly invite you to become a member of our private sync club called The Sync Society. We're a welcoming bunch, generously sharing our experiences in sync and advice. The spirit of this book drives what we do with it. You can find details on our incredibly valuable club that you can join here: 2Indie.com/SyncSociety

When you're ready to start pitching your music, 2Indie hosts a conference every year that allows you to meet dozens of the top sync agencies in the world live via online video. It includes Q&A and listening sessions. Definitely consider this conference. It's the perfect way to get to know a lot of agencies in a short period of time, and then use that experience to narrow down your initial list of agencies to reach out to. You'll also meet hundreds of other indie music makers that you can network and potentially collaborate with. To keep in the loop on when it's being offered make sure you are on our email list and you can always visit 2Indie.com to see what is happening.

Looking forward to hearing about where your sync journey leads you. Keep us posted along the way, we always love hearing from you: way@2indie.com

John & Sonnet

ABOUT THE AUTHORS

About John Clinebell

Nashville-based Producer/Songwriter John Clinebell's music has been heard by millions around the world. Placements include major networks and brands like FOX, Disney/ABC, CBS, BET, ESPN, Nick Jr, Netflix, Hulu, Facebook/Instagram, Starbucks, and PrettyLittleThing. Former VP of Music with licensing agency Catch The Moon, he's the co-founder of the music business education company 2Indie. 2Indie is on a mission to make career fulfillment possible for all music makers. Through coaching, podcasting, and as an author, John's helped thousands of indie artists to "flip the switch from learning to earning" in the music industry. He's also a yogi, gamer, 1980s enthusiast, and former dodgeball champion!

About Sonnet Simmons

Los Angeles-based Singer/Songwriter Sonnet Simmons' heart-opening voice and original music has been heard by millions around the world with hundreds of placements in ads such as Coca-Cola, Volkswagen, GoDaddy, Nivea, T-Mobile, Microsoft, Nike, Starbucks, Reebok, Lee Jeans, and TV shows like Younger, Riverdale, Katy Keene and many more. Former VP of music licensing company Catch The Moon, Sonnet was responsible for pitching a catalog of music and landing placements for many other indie artists to find sync success with brands such as McDonald's, MaxMara, Nordstrom, Tommy Hilfiger, and more.

Sonnet first garnered the love of America as one of the top contestants on ABC's Rising Star with Josh Groban, Kesha, Ludacris, and Brad Paisley.

Sonnet has been a music business coach since 2016, helping thousands of indie artists, singers, songwriters, and producers around the world find success in sync. She co-founded the music business education company 2Indie. 2Indie is on a mission to make career fulfillment possible for all music makers. Born in Athens, Greece, she grew up in Los Angeles, where she is now raising her two adorable toddlers.

About Josh Young
Josh Young, founder and CEO of Atrium Music, is a three-time Emmy-nominated supervising television and film editor whose vision for a better media brand of music library birthed Atrium Music. Atrium Music is a publishing and music library that licenses and places music in television, film, and commercial productions.

Josh is driven by his passion to separate himself and Atrium from other companies and has built Atrium as a company rooted in brand integrity and passion. By bridging the gap between creative and business, Atrium allows "artists to be artists" while allowing the business structure of Atrium to handle their business needs. Over 900 artists and composers have found a home with Atrium and the vast pool of composers and content producers signed to Atrium surrounds the globe. Atrium's goal is to place its fingerprint on the world with its music and business ethics, and has done so in 87 countries.

When not producing, editing, or music supervising nationally syndicated television shows, Josh is relentless in growing and sharing his personal industry experiences. Josh actively attends and speaks at conferences and educational institutions across the US. He is an active participant on panels of industry discussions throughout the United States: Summer and Winter NAMM, Durango, Sync Summit, Musicians Institute, Citrus College, West Coast Songwriters, Far-West, Sync Summit, The CCC, MusExpo, NAB, AVID, 2Indie's Get Repped! and many more. Josh has sat on the board for West Coast Songwriters and is currently an active board member for the California Copyright Conference.

THANK YOU, THANK YOU, THANK YOU!

We could not have created this book without the help of our dear friends, family, and colleagues in the sync industry. And to Alessandra Simmons for helping with edits. Thank you from the bottom of our hearts!

From John and Sonnet:
The entire 2Indie community (that we are so blessed to serve), all of our students and colleagues from the Catch The Moon days, Josh Young, Alec Stern, Billy Lefler, Cathy Heller, Kirstin VanLandingham, Kari Kimmel, Drew Sherrod, Kristina Benson, Mike Soens, Cinder Ernst, Elisa Share, Chris TY Avery, Moe Loughran, Sam Knaak, Nick Phelps, Mary Haller, Rebecca Trujillo Vest, Marci Elizabeth, John "X" Volaitis, Kimera Morrell, Mariana Risquez, Kurt Hunter, Kara Jones, Mark Wilder, Kat Kennedy, Brad Cryan, Will Chadwick, John Newcomer, Wendy Parr, Shannon Palazzolo, Brett Byrd,

Dan Waldkirch, Jacob Piontek, Annie Pearlman, Clancy Magnuson, Katy McIlvaine, Bria Dunlap, Sierra Jordan, Doug Darnell, Ryan M. Carroll, Natalie Becker, John Anderson, Patrick Hughes, Alexis Colson, Rashad Richardson, Jenè Etheridge, Brian Vickers, Jennifer Smith, Alex Stacey, Gary Calamar, Mike Turner, Crystal Grooms Mangano, Jennifer Mandel, Brian Naguit, Madonna Wade-Reed, James Combs, Ann Kline, Kelsey Mitchell, Sarah Chapeck, Armine Ramer, Nick Maker, Jordan Young, Gregory Sweeney, Mike Ladman, Adèle Ho, Rosie Howe, Adele Ho, Ryan Gaines, Rinat Arinos, Melissa Aubert, Kayla Masnek, Michael Fey, Staci Slater, MUNNYCAT, Kyle Langlois, Meagan Geer, Eddy Bishai, Joey Plunkett, Amira Gadd, Gabrielle Taryn, Dianna St. Hillaire, Christiana Sudano, Eric Campbell, Kristin Summers, Jarrod Ward, Spencer Ludwig, Elaine Ryan, Tamara Bubble, Glory Reinstein, Celia Rose, Mariela Arredondo, Pei Pei, and Dalaina Knight.

From John:

I wanna first start by thanking Sonnet Simmons, who puts up with all my never-ending crazy new ideas for 2Indie. You encourage the very best in me, and I am constantly inspired by your genuine kindness and unwavering desire to show up and help others. I'm so thankful for the real wisdom and heart you added to this book. Thanks to my grandpa, Lyle Ray Clinebell, and grandma, Helen Louise Kimmel Clinebell, who were the most supportive and loving people I've ever known.

Thanks to my dad, James Ronald Clinebell, who started writing several fascinating books during his lifetime (about education, philosophy, and rambling around the Western U.S. as a folk troubadour in his V.W. bus during the early '70s) but never finished or published any. Thanks to Billy Lefler, who has taught me so much, but perhaps most importantly that you don't need to stop having fun to be successful in life. Thanks to Cathy Heller for teaching me to fish in sync. You helped me stand up for my dreams, and hired me for the most amazing job - coaching at (and helping run) Catch The Moon Music. I'm so grateful for it all. Big thanks to all of my brothers from another mother - you know who you are! I have so many more thanks to list out than is possible, but I'm gonna try now. Thanks to Clay Campbell, Alessio Miraglia, Stefano Bussadori, Bryan Neustein, John Wolf, Felix Bollinger, Adrianne Gonzalez, Scott Cresto, Dario Forzato, Eddie Wohl, Al Machera, Asher Condit, Kris Bradley, Luke Tozour, Shay Watson, Jean Catchings, Ceri Earle, Uncle Jeff & Aunt Shan, Uncle Dana & Aunt Vicki, grandma & grandpa Winslow, Willow Stephens, Tom Verrette, Kimi Lundy Liope, Nonseq, Gary King, Maya La Maya, Adrian Alvarado, Alex Bradfield, Steve Collom, Emily Anderson, Anelda & Sean Spence, Rora Wilde, Shanin Blake, K.P. Wolfe, Joh Chase, Caleb Conner, Chelsea Davis, Levi Downey, Ben Drysdale, Lindsay Garfield, Shani Rose Kfir, Mitchell Kilpatrick, Danielle Hollobaugh, Callie Galvez, Chelsea Aguilar, Sacha, Melinda, Sean, Brandon, Ri, Princess Superstar, Jason Lowrie, Jared Lindbloom, Teresa

Wright, Peter Brynjolfson, Tim Malugin, Richard Dillon, Kat McDowell, Jon Sorensen, Heidi Webster, Elddy Trevino, all of my haters, all of my collaborators, and all my old dodgeball and yoga friends in L.A.

From Sonnet:
Truly, there is no end to my gratitude. I have the world to thank. You, the reader, and our beautiful community. Thank you. As it pertains to this book, I'd like to take a second to highlight a few individuals. Thank you to my biz partner, John Clinebell for having so much integrity, dreaming and scheming new ways to show up in this world bigger and better, and making this book a possibility. To Cathy Heller, who lit a fire of my own power inside of me, who taught me what is possible for this life, who gave me the reins to her music licensing company, which gave me a chance to fly in sync, and still to this day, shows us all what is true through her example. Thank you to my mom, sis, and bro, family, and best friends, for holding me to my authenticity and cheering for my dreams. Every co-writer, producer, publisher, agency, and Supe I know and have worked with, for being the wild pieces that make the puzzle of my teams and this industry life we share. To Billy Lefler for hearing me, seeing me, and helping me bring my music to the public again with this last record. For my family who light up my every day with laughter and purpose and motivate me to be the best version of myself and be an example of not giving up on my dreams.

SYNC LICENSING AGENCY DIRECTORY

This is far from a comprehensive list, but feel free to use this list as a starting point to conduct your research.

411 Music Group
A&G Sync Music
Atrium Music
Bank Robber Music
Crucial Music
Dawn Patrol Music
Echoette
Friendly Fire Licensing
Ghostwriter Music
Glow Music Group
Heavy Hitters Music
Imaginary Friends Music Partners
Kobalt Music
Koze Music

Lo Fi Music

Lyric House

Madden Flow Entertainment

Marmoset

Melody Haunts Reverie

Music Alternatives

Mutiny Recordings

Peermusic

PEN Music Group

Pink Shark Music

Position Music

Robot Repair

Secret Road

Shoot The Noise

Song And Film

SoStereo

Steven Scharf Entertainment

Sugaroo!

Sweet On Top

Sync Daddy

The Talent House

Think Music

Triple Scoop Music

Truly Music

Vision Works Music

Zync Music

Sync Educator / Agencies
Blue Buddha Entertainment

For Goodness Sync

HD Music Now

Sus3 Music

twoOhsix Music

Unicorn Sync

What Up Pitches

Production Music Libraries / Publishers
APM

Audio Network

Black Toast Music

BMG Production Music

Howling Music

Jingle Punks

Megatrax

Spirit Music Group

Universal Production Music

VideoHelper

Warner Chappell Music

Royalty-Free / Stock Libraries
Artlist

Audiosocket

Audiosparx

Audio Jungle

Epidemic Sound

Filmstro

Hooksounds

Musicbed

Music Gateway

Music Vine

Pond5

PremiumBeat

Songtradr

Soundstripe

Uppbeat

TOP THEMES FOR SYNC SONGWRITING

We've created this comprehensive list of sync themes to help inspire you in your writing sessions and understand the types of songs most frequently asked for in sync licensing requests (briefs). These are loosely listed in the order in which we see demand for them, but definitely don't sleep on the entire list.

1. Platonic Love / Friends / You've Got A Friend
2. Overcoming Obstacles
3. Empowerment / Swagger / Express Yourself
4. Together / In This Together / Unity / Teamwork
5. Home / Coming Home
6. Family
7. Happy / Happiness / Feeling Good
8. Now / In The Moment / Carpe Diem / Seize The Day
9. Do / Do It / Let's Do This
10. Yeah / Yes / Okay / Uh Huh / Oh Yeah

11. Christmas / Holiday Music
12. We Got It All / It's All Here / We Got You
13. Good Life / It's Good
14. New / Brand New / New Day / New World
15. Believe / Inspiring / It's Possible
16. Dreams / Imagination
17. Improvement / Upgrade / Level Up / Better
18. I Like It / I Love It / I Need It / I Want It
19. Greatness / Success / Being The Best / Achievement
20. Hero / I'll Save The Day / Rising To The Challenge / Over Impossible Odds
21. Unstoppable / Invincible / Unbreakable
22. Bold / High Impact / Striking
23. Perfect / Perfection
24. Beauty / Beautiful
25. Rebel / Renegade / Break The Rules / Change The Game
26. Change / Change Things Up / Transform
27. Free / Freedom / Carefree / Living Free
28. Being Young / New Generation / Youth
29. Summertime / Sun / Sunshine
30. Party / Get The Party Started / Let's Party / Have A Good Time / Have Fun / Cut Loose / Celebrate
31. Pure Evil / The Devil / Twisted
32. Secrets / Skeletons in the Closet
33. Go / Move
34. Fast / Faster / High Speed

35. Exploration / Adventure / Discovery
36. Travel / Get Away
37. Betrayal
38. Romantic Love / Young Love / Teenage Love
39. Luxury / Class / Timeless / Timelessness
40. Good Old Days / Looking Back Fondly / Better With Age / Best Days

COMPREHENSIVE SYNC GLOSSARY

Act - A section of a trailerized composition that includes the build all the way through the crescendo it builds up towards. Typically trailer music contains three distinct acts.

Ad Agency - An advertising company that works with brands and brand agencies to develop effective media campaigns. These can include commercials in print, television, and online.

Admin Deal / Pub Admin Deal - When a songwriter contracts with a publishing administrator to collect their performance royalties. The benefit to this can be that if the songwriter has music generating royalties worldwide, the publisher will likely be able to collect more of that money than the songwriter can by self-publishing. This is due to the complexity of comprehensively collecting performance royalties internationally.

Administration - The work required to legally protect and make money from your songs. This can include registering your music with a PRO, filing copyrights, and taking in various fees and royalties and distributing them. Specific to music licensing, the term "admin" can also refer to the management of a library of music which includes both the sound files and metadata associated with them.

Administrator - Someone who has been tasked with the administration of a collection of songs. This can be an individual or an entity such as a publishing company. Indie artists often are the sole administrators of their music.

All In - Refers to "both sides" of a master sync fee. Master sync fees are split evenly between two sides, the master rights holders and publishing rights holders. When a quoted fee is "all in," it means the amount quoted is the total amount given for both sides added together.

Alt - A song written and produced to closely match the genre and vibe of a targeted reference track, done without violating the copyright of it. Alt can also be used to describe a song that takes a unique twist on a popular genre such as "Alt R&B" or "Alt Gospel."

Alt Mixes / Submixes - Stereo mixes of a recorded song that can provide alternatives to whomever is looking to use the song for a media project. An example of a common alt mix is a "TV Track" (or "Performance Track") which is the main mix of a song minus only the lead vocal.

Anthemic - A way of describing strong, uplifting music with lyrics that reinforce a popularly held conviction. Typically anthemic songs include sudden and dramatic changes in dynamics (they "explode" into the chorus). Anthemic themes are celebratory in nature.

Arranger - The person who creatively directs how a written song (or section of a song) is performed. They determine what instruments play what parts, as well as the relationship they have with each other. This term can be used in the contexts of both live shows and studio recordings. It can mean working with live instrument or vocal parts, completely digital instruments, or a combination of all of them.

Assignment of Copyright - When copyright of a song is transferred to a new owner. Must be legally done in writing.

Audio/Visual Work - The visual portion of a work that accompanies sound. Can be film, TV, slideshows, video games, commercials, etc.

Backend - A popular term used to describe the performance royalties a music creator receives from their PRO. When talking about payment for a TV placement, people will commonly refer to "the backend" as the money they will get after the show airs.

Background Instrumental - In sync context, this refers to a use of an instrumental section of a song to picture (vs. using a section with vocals). Often specified in master sync agreements and quote requests.

Background Score - Typically instrumental music that is custom composed to support a TV or film scene. This can also be previously composed instrumental music that is licensed from a composer or library.

Background Vocal - In sync context, this refers to a use of a vocal section of a song to picture (vs. using the instrumental). Often specified in master sync agreements and quote requests.

Bed Track - The foundation of a song. It can be the rhythm and chord structure.

Blanket License - Music libraries and publishers can strike blanket license deals that open their entire (often easily searchable) catalog of songs to a production company to use for a set rate.

BPM - Stands for "beats per minute." It's one of the ways you can measure the tempo (speed) of a song. This is a piece of metadata you will want to include and encode into your mastered sound files.

Brand Agency - An agency that specializes in helping companies or entities solidify their branding. This can range from support in understanding your brand, your audience, clarifying your goals and how to communicate best with your audience to achieve these goals to help you tell your story and grow your brand.

Brief - Music supervisors send out "briefs" to trusted publishers and rep agencies describing the specific kinds of songs they need for the media projects they are currently working on. Rep agencies may also send out briefs to their artist roster requesting songs on behalf of their music supervisor network.

Broadcast Producer (more commonly known as **Integrated Producer**) - They work at ad agencies and often work with brand agencies and their clients to create a musical vision, tone and style that best suits a particular advertising campaign. They then legally deliver all the music needed for the project within the budgetary constraints.

Broadcast Quality - A way of describing songs that are recorded professionally, and are therefore "radio ready." It can also refer to the 24 bit/48Khz broadcast quality standard for high-fidelity song recording masters.

Build - A part of a song that builds up tension and excitement over time.

Bumper - A short piece of music used to help transition between two scenes or programming segments. One example is the music you hear going into or heading back from commercials.

Buyout - Like with a Work For Hire, this is where someone pays to own the copyright of someone's musical works. Often with a buyout both the copyrights to the song itself and the song recording are purchased outright.

Catalog - Also referred to as a library. It's a collection of songs.

Cinematic / Orchestral - A way of describing music that powerfully incorporates orchestral instruments and arrangements into it. Cinematic songs can feel trailerized, building up in separate "acts" to a massive crescendo towards the end.

Clearance - The legal process which allows copyrighted music to be used in a media project. A song must be "cleared" first in order to be legally used in an ad, TV show or film.

Confirmation Letter / License Request - A letter from a music supervisor confirming the terms agreed upon in the quote request letter. This also includes any changes to the terms like the final timing or fee for the song use. This often serves as the final license for independent artists. It can be a formal legal document or simply an email confirming your song's use in a project.

Content ID - Digital fingerprinting system developed by Google which is used to easily identify and manage copyrighted content on YouTube. Songs can get flagged by Content ID for being used without authorization in videos. In those cases, the copyright holders of the songs in question can deny use or allow it under fair use.

Context - The specific way a song is being used in a media project. One of the key drivers of performance royalty fees in sync. Typically the more involved/important the context, the higher the fees that are paid by the PROs.

Copyright - The exclusive legal right, given to an originator or an assignee to print, publish, perform, film, or record literary, artistic, or musical material, and to authorize others to do the same. *(Oxford Dictionary)*

Cover - A new recording of a previously released song from another artist.

Cue - The location in a media project where a piece of music is (or will be) placed. Can also refer to the piece of music itself that is placed.

Cue Sheet - An important document submitted to PROs by whoever is responsible for song clearance for a media project. That person is typically the music supervisor. The cue sheet is a comprehensive list of the music contained in a media program (TV program or film) and is necessary for the

PROs to have in order to properly distribute performance royalties to rights holders.

Custom Songs - Songs composed to match the exact needs of a specific media project. For example, a Coca-Cola ad might want a song for a commercial that includes keywords or phrases that directly match what is happening on screen.

Derivative Work - A new version of an existing song. Only the copyright owner can significantly alter a song or use it as part of a new song. This is different from a cover, this means you are taking a previously written song and using parts or all of it to compose your own new song. It's not allowed under copyright law without the permission of the copyright owner.

Direct License - When a song's rights holders directly license their performance rights with a business entity, circumventing the PROs. This can only be done if you are with an American PRO, and it requires notifying your PRO so they don't attempt to collect performance royalties from the business entity that has directly licensed the music. An example of this would be if a self-published American artist directly licensed a song to a company providing music to a department store chain for their in-store play.

DISCO - Industry standard software for music licensing professionals to manage their song libraries. In one place, one can upload all their sound files, encode metadata into them, create relevant tags/keywords for them, and embed lyrics and artwork. DISCO makes it easy to organize, search and share songs.

Drop - A sonic and emotional payoff in a song. Typically used to describe the moment a big chorus hits.

Dynamics / Dynamic Range - Used to describe the difference in loudness between sections of a song. For example, if a song has a lot of dynamics, it has both louder and quieter sections to the arrangement. In licensing, having contrasting dynamics in your song can really help support changes being depicted in a scene.

Duration - Seen on both licensing agreements and cue sheets. The total length of time a music cue plays in a media project. This includes the exact number of minutes and seconds.

Easy Clearance - A term used to describe a song that is easy for a music supervisor (or other decision maker) to secure the synchronization rights to. Typically songs that are "easy clears" are both one stop and affordable to license.

Edit Point - A point in a song that works well to edit it to picture. This can be an existing break in the song, or one that is created by an editor using the stems.

ENO Insurance - This is short for "Errors & Omissions Insurance." Large agencies and production houses always have this insurance that protects them in case a song that they use for a media project isn't properly cleared. It can protect them (and their clients) against the impact of lawsuits for infringement of copyright.

Ephemeral Use - A set of circumstances where copyrighted music can be used in live TV and radio broadcasts without securing a license. These free uses typically only apply to the initial airing. An example of this would be someone having a copyrighted song audibly playing in their car while being interviewed by a TV reporter.

EQ - Short for equalize, which means adjust the frequencies of a sound or song. Using a plug-in to boost low frequencies and cut high frequencies of a kick drum track is just one example of EQ. EQ can be used to creative effect on individual elements in a mix or the entire mix itself.

Exclusive - Granting exclusive permission. Commonly used in rep agreements, publishing agreements, and song licenses to define an exclusive relationship or use.

Exploitation - Using a composition and/or master to make money.

External Use - Refers to use of a copyrighted song song in any non-broadcast medium to any individual or audience that is not a member of the company or organization licensing the use. This may include public events, fundraisers, sales meetings, or tradeshow displays.

Fair Use - A legal doctrine that promotes freedom of expression by permitting the unlicensed use of copyright-protected works in certain circumstances. Placing a copyrighted song in a media project intended for commercial purposes is *never* considered fair use.

Finder's Fee - In music licensing, this is a fee given to someone who helps another person (or company) find a song they need for a media project. The person receiving the finder's fee has acted as an intermediary and has reached a business agreement to be compensated for their efforts.

Genre - The categorical description of a style of music. Popular genres include hip-hop, pop, and singer/songwriter.

Groove - The propulsive feel of a beat pattern in music. Describing the groove of a song is more about how a beat makes you feel than a technical description of a song's rhythm.

HFA - Short for "Harry Fox Agency." They issue the necessary mechanical licenses needed by artists that wish to record and release covers.

Hook - Many modern recording studios refer to song choruses as "the hook." It's often the catchiest part of the song. However the term "hook" can also be used interchangeably to simply mean a catchy instrumental or vocal melody that repeats.

Impact - A dramatic rhythmic and/or melodic sound that hits suddenly then rings out to emphasize a transition in music. Can combine low frequency and high frequency sounds to create an impact. Commonly used in trailer music.

In Context / Out Of Context - "In Context" means the specific scene for which a song has been granted a sync license for. Any other scene or use would be considered "Out of Context." These are separate rights often specified in a music licensing agreement.

In Perpetuity - Forever! In licensing, when this term is included the term of the licensing agreement never ends.

In The Box - Music production, mixing and/or mastering done using only a computer and its software. "In the box" also can refer to productions that are *mostly* done without the use of external hardware like a microphone, preamp, etc.

Indie - Short for "independent artist," someone not signed to a major record label or publisher.

Infringement - Violating the copyright of someone's song or song recording. This usually means the infringer has unlawfully copied creative ideas directly from copyrighted materials.

Instrumentals - Songs without vocals. They can be original instrumental works, or a mix of a vocal song without the vocals. Instrumental versions are often included when a song with vocals is being pitched.

Integrated Producer / Broadcast Producer - They work at Ad Agencies and often work with Brand Agencies and their clients to create a musical vision, tone and style that best suits a particular advertising campaign. They then legally deliver all the music needed for the project within the budgetary constraints.

Internal Use / Corporate Use - This is a type of music license where a song is used in a media project that is created for and only viewed by members of a specific company or organization. An example of this would be licensing a song for use in a corporate training video.

ISRC - Stands for "International STandard Recording Code." An internationally unique identifier for sound recordings, ISRC codes play a vital role in tracking music that is commercially distributed. When you DIY release a song, your distributor typically assigns an ISRC code to it.

Keywords - in metadata helps the user know what to expect from the song in terms of lyrical themes, genres, searchable info and data, and categorize music by keywords.

Letter of Direction - What a publisher sends to a PRO when they are taking over administrative control of a songwriter's registered works. This is how a publisher starts collecting performance royalties on behalf of a songwriter.

Library - A collection of songs. Also referred to as a catalog.

License - An agreement where the owners of musical works are compensated for certain uses of their work in exchange for limited rights to use the work by a purchaser. The creators of films, TV shows and ad campaigns will often license copyrighted music to include in their projects. In order to legally do that, a license must be agreed to and executed. In the industry, this term is commonly interchangeable with "sync license," "sync" and "placement."

License Fee - The "up front" fee given by the Licensee to the Licensor to license their song. Does not refer to any backend fees.

Licensee - The person or business entity licensing a recorded song.

Licensor - The person or business entity who legally represents (and therefore can grant a license to) a recorded song.

Loop - A repeating musical section in a song. In modern production, loops are often seamlessly repeated in an arrangement to create a beat (or part of one).

Lyrical Theme - The subject of a song's lyrics. Songs can contain one or many themes. In sync, lyrical themes are important because often what is being depicted on screen needs a song with a specific lyrical theme to help support it.

Lyrics - The words of a song.

Lyric Ups - When the vocals are up on a song that's set to picture. This commonly happens in montage sequences on TV shows and films.

Master - A recorded piece of music. Can also be referred to as "sound recording" and "master recording."

Mastering - The last step in audio production, mastering is the creative and technical process by which a final song mix is prepared for broadcast. The enhancements in sound are usually done by a mastering engineer after the mixer is done, though with indie artists sometimes the mixer is also the mastering engineer.

Master Fee - The up-front money given to the master owners of a sound recording by the purchaser who wishes to license the song for their media project.

Mechanical Rights - The legal rights to reproduce a recorded song. Songwriters and producers are paid mechanical royalties by distributors/labels per song purchased (on vinyl, CD or cassette), downloaded and/or streamed on digital platforms.

Mechanical Royalties - Payments sent to songwriters and producers by distributors/labels when their songs are purchased (on vinyl, CD or cassette), downloaded and/or streamed on digital platforms.

Media Rights Requested - The legal specification of where a media project (that a licensed song is contained in) will be distributed. "All media now known or hereafter devised" is often used to clear all forms of media in current use and any that are invented in the future. Some agreements specify a narrower use such as "Internet Streaming Only."

Metadata - The set of data that can be encoded into audio files. Metadata can help a person determine important facts about the music. Information commonly included are the song title, artist, genre, label, and a comments field. The comments field in metadata is often used to include the songwriting/master splits and contact information for who can clear the song for licensing purposes. *Note: as far as popular audio file formats in sync go, only AIFF and MP3 files can have metadata encoded into them.*

Mix - Mixing is the creative process through which an engineer uses a variety of tools and techniques to adjust all of the individual tracks of a studio recording in order to achieve a professional sound. A "mix" is the stereo audio file that results from that process.

Most Favored Nations (MFN) Clause - If a music licensing contract has language in it that requires MFN, it means that all songs for a particular film or show episode must be paid the same licensing fee. In this way, all songs (and their rights holders) are treated as the "most favored."

Music Library - Companies that represent big catalogs of music that have been created for the sole purpose of landing sync licenses. They help decision makers in media projects find the music they need and quickly clear it for use. Some music libraries are niche, while the major ones represent just about any genre of music you can imagine.

Music Licensing - Music licensing is the licensed use of copyrighted music. Music licensing is intended to ensure that the owners of copyrights on musical works are compensated for certain uses of their work.

Music Coordinator - Support and serve a media project under the Music Supervisor. They often contribute creatively, but also do the important work needed to negotiate deals and clear music used on a media project.

Music Publishing - Music publishing is the business of promotion and monetization of musical works: music publishers make sure that songwriters receive royalties for their compositions, and also work to generate opportunities for the songwriters and their music.

Music Supervisor - They work with a project's production team to determine the musical vision, tone and style that best suits the media project. They then legally deliver all the music needed for the project within the budgetary constraints. They are part DJ, part negotiator, part detective, and part magician!

Musical Work / Musical Composition - An original piece of music. This can be with or without vocals.

Musicologist - An academic expert in music. In sync, musicologists are often consulted when stakeholders need to identify any potential music copyright violation concerns with songs they place in media projects.

Master Sync Fee - The upfront sync fee for the "Master" or sound recording portion of the song.

Media - Mass audio/visual communication. Forms of media include broadcast television, film, video games, and podcasts.

Needle Drops - Slang for single sync licenses of single songs in a show or film. If there are 12 different songs being used on a TV show, that constitutes 12 needle drops. This language is often used in the context of discussing whether a show or film is using music library pulls or not (music library pulls are not considered needle drops).

Neighboring Rights - Public performance royalties due to sound recording copyright holders. These are different royalties than those collected by PROs. They are paid to master owners and artists of a song, not the songwriting and publishing owners. The U.S. does not recognize neighboring rights because their radio stations do not pay royalties to recording owners and performing artists. However, services like SoundExchange can still collect neighboring rights from online and satellite radio platforms like Pandora and Sirius.

One Stop - If you are authorized to represent all assignable rights to a song for sync, then that means you are the "One-Stop Shop" for that track. This means that 100% of the publishing and master rights are completely cleared in advance. Having your songs be one stop is highly desirable in the licensing world because it makes things so much easier for whoever is looking to clear the song. They won't have to track down and clear rights with multiple different rights holders.

One Stop Agreement - Remember, if a piece of music is a "one stop" clearance, it means someone who is trying to license a track only has to contact one party to clear both the Master and Publishing Rights. A one stop agreement is when all of the owners of the master and publishing rights to a song agree to allow one or multiple parties to represent all of the rights to the song. This can facilitate faster deals in music licensing when one or more parties can quickly authorize a media use without needing to first confer with all the rights owners of the song.

Orphan Works - When a copyright owner to a song can't be identified or located, making the song impossible to license.

Performance Royalties - Royalties paid to songwriters and publishers for the right to publicly use copyrighted music. This includes live shows, in-store, TV and radio broadcasts and interactive digital streaming. Performance royalties are collected from public users by PROs on behalf of songwriters and their publishers.

Performing Rights Organization (PRO) - Also referred to as "collection societies," these organizations collect performance royalties on behalf of songwriters and their publishers. The three biggest PROs for songwriters and publishers in the U.S. are ASCAP, BMI and SESAC. It's important to have your songs registered with a PRO so that you collect all the performance royalties due to you when a song is placed in a media project.

Placement - See **License.**

Post Production - The stage in the production of a media project where the sound and picture are edited together.

Pre-Clear - When the potential licensor of a song comes to a preliminary agreement with the copyright holders for use of their song in a media project. Music supervisors, for example, will frequently pre-clear music they wish to use in a project with the parties who control all the rights needed to authorize its use. This is done ahead of time to speed up the clearance process.

Producer - The music industry's equivalent of a film director, the music producer is the creative and technical leader of a project. They oversee the production of records, working closely with a project's artist to bring a common sonic vision to life.

Production Coordinator - In the advertising world, they support and serve Integrated/Broadcast Producers (much in the same way that Music Coordinators serve a Music Supervisor). They often contribute creatively, but also can do the important work needed to negotiate deals and clear music used on a media project.

Production Music - Also referred to as stock music or library music. This is previously recorded music represented by music libraries for easy clearance in film, television, and other media.

Public Domain - Songs that have no copyright owner, and therefore are not protected by copyright law. Anyone can use a public domain song without anyone's permission, but no one can own it. Songs typically enter the public domain when their copyrights expire, around 70 years after the original songwriter's death.

Publisher - A person or company who works on behalf of the songwriters they contract with to collect and pay out all of the performance royalties they earn from their music. Depending on the scope of the deal, they may also enforce copyrights, set up creative collaborations, and pitch for licensing opportunities.

Publisher Shares / Publishing - The legal rights attributed to the publisher of a song. The income for a copyrighted composition is divided equally between the songwriters and publishers. The publisher share is the side owed to publishers.

Pull Bin / Selects - The audio file folder that video editors pull their music from to use in the edit. It's often filled with temp music that the editor has chosen for the media project.

Quote Request Letter - The first formal step in clearing a song. It's a simple legal document that details how a production company wishes to use your song, the songwriting and master splits, and how much they will pay. While not a final license, it is only sent out if the media project is serious about using your song. They will sometimes ask you to fill out the amount (you give them a quote), but with indies a lot of the time they will tell you how much budget they have available to clear the song and the request document will already have the amount written in. Once the quote request is signed and sent back, the production company has pre-cleared the song for use based on the agreed upon terms.

References - In terms of music licenses, this refers to the songs a songwriter referred to for inspiration for their composition.

Registration - Registering your songs with a PRO or copyright office.

Rep Agency / Licensing Agency - A company that represents artists and composers for the specific purpose of pitching their music for licensing opportunities.

Rep Agreement - Agreement between rep company and artist/composer to represent their music for pitching for music licensing opportunities.

Reference Track - A song chosen as songwriting or production inspiration for the creation of a new song. Reference tracks are also often used when mixing and mastering to compare a work-in-progress with a finished professional product.

Retitling - When a composition is registered with a PRO under a new title. This is typically done so that the company registering the new title of the composition can keep performance royalties it collects separate from those of the original registration of the song.

Riser - A sound that gradually increases in volume, pitch or a combination of parameters. Typically used to build tension up in a production.

Royalty Free Music / Libraries - Companies who offer affordable music to license to content creators. Often they will have an easily searchable library of many different genres of music. Typically a user pays an up-front fee to the company in exchange for a blanket license to use the paid-for song however they see fit, with some exceptions. Royalty free libraries serve everyone from couples looking for music for their wedding video to indie filmmakers and production companies.

SAG Royalties - Residual payments due to actors from the Screen Actors Guild for uses of performances on film and television that go beyond the fees already paid to them. In sync, there are some cases where a musical artist or performer can qualify for SAG royalties.

Sample - A part of an existing piece of recorded music used in a new work. In sync, all samples must be legally cleared in order for a song to be used to picture.

Sample Clearance - The process of obtaining legal permission from copyright owners to use a sample of their recorded work in a new work.

Scene Description - The specific description of the use of a song to picture. This language is included in master sync agreements and quote requests to state exactly what the song is being cleared for.

Schedule A - The complete list of songs included in a rep deal.

Self-Publishing - When an indie artist sets up a publishing account with their PRO so they can register the publishing for their own songs. That way they can collect publishing performance royalties due to them through their PRO.

188 | Get Signed In Sync

Side / Half - In a master sync deal, the fee is split between the master recording and the publishing. These constitute the two "sides" of the fee being paid to clear the song. Negotiations will often refer to sides of a song, or "all in" which is the combined fee.

Single Use - A license where a song is only used once in one scene of a media project.

Sizzle - A network TV promo that previews the upcoming season of programming.

Songwriter - A person who creatively contributes to writing a song. This can involve the lyrics, melody, arrangement, structure, or all of the above. "Songwriter" is also used to legally define the person or entity that owns the songwriting rights to a composition.

Songwriter Shares / Songwriting - The legal rights attributed to the writer/composer of a song. The income for a copyrighted composition is divided equally between the songwriters and publishers. The songwriter share is the side owed to songwriters.

Sound Recording - A recorded piece of music. Commonly referred to as "master" or "master recording."

Source Cue / Source Music - The music being played in a media scene from a source shown (or implied). For example, in a bar scene there might be a jukebox in the corner. The music playing from that jukebox would be considered source music. Another example is a scene of someone walking through a dorm hallway. One of the doors is open and you hear music coming from inside the room. That's also source music.

Split Sheet - An agreement between music creators that specifies what percentage of the songwriting and master rights to a particular work each of them own. These percentages are important because they determine how much each songwriter and master owner will be paid when income is generated by their music.

Splits - How the rights to a song and/or song recording are divided between copyright owners. In sync, splits determine who earns money and how much of it when a song is placed.

Stabs - Staccato notes that add dramatic emphasis to a recorded song.

Stems - Stems are the complete collection of stereo mixes of all the different parts of your song. For example, a drum stem will usually be a stereo audio file that includes all the drums of your song and nothing more. A typical song will have a few different stems including drums, bass, vocals, background vocals, keyboards, guitars, percussion, etc. These are the building blocks that a film or TV editor might need to create a custom-tailored alternate mix of your song that works perfectly to the scene on screen.

Sting / Sounder - A short piece of music (up to 15 seconds long) that succinctly ends. Typically used to punctuate the beginnings and ends of media productions, with voiceover laid in over the top of it. A stinger is often a submix of a longer cue in a music library.

Sub-Publisher - Someone who acts as an agent to a publisher's catalog. They collect royalties, administer copyrights and clear songs for licensing use on behalf of the publisher. When a sub-publisher is present, they are registered with the PROs so that they can directly collect performance royalties. If media projects that use your music have a popular worldwide distribution, a reputable sub-publisher may be able to collect substantial international royalties for you that you would otherwise not collect from your PRO when you self-publish.

Super Tease - A promo that teases an entire season of a television show. It hypes up the show and gives the audience an idea of what to expect to happen.

Swagger - A way of describing high energy songs with heavy impact and boldly positive attitude. Typically swagger songs are in-your-face and unrelenting once they get going.

Sync Fee - The up-front money paid to the copyright owners of a song used in a media project such as a television show or film.

Synchronization License (or "Sync") - A music synchronization license, or "sync" for short, is a music license granted by the holder of the copyright of a particular composition, allowing the licensee to synchronize ("sync") music with some kind of visual media output (film, television shows, advertisements, video games, movie trailers, etc.).

Temp Music / Temp Track - Music temporarily put into a TV show or film scene by an editor. This often happens before any clearance work for the music is done. Sometimes it's only put in there to give ideas to the director, composer and/or music supervisor.

Term - The period of time a license is in effect. Music licensing agreements should always have this clearly stated.

Territory - The geographical area of the world in which a contract (such as a music license) is valid.

The Mechanical Collective (MLC): A nonprofit organization that administers blanket mechanical licenses to some U.S. streaming services (such as Spotify), and pays royalties to songwriters, composers, lyricists, and music publishers that come from these blanket licenses.

Timing - The specific amount of time a song is being used to picture.

Topline - The lyrics and vocal melody of a song. Topliners are writers who add the lyrics and vocal melody to an instrumental track to create a completed vocal song.

Underscore - Music used underneath dialogue in a TV or film scene.

Universal - If the theme and story of a song is broad and general enough to work to picture in many different situations, it's considered universal. Universal lyrics and the songs they are contained in tend to focus on common emotions that most people can strongly relate to.

Visual Instrumental - A use where an instrumental song is performed on camera. This includes a character playing just the guitar in a scene, a live band, etc.

Visual Vocal - A use where a vocal song is performed on camera. This includes a character humming a song in a scene, a live concert, etc.

Work-For-Hire - A paid job where the musical talent retains no rights to the product they worked on. Under a WFH agreement, the employer owns the copyrights to all creative contributions of the employee to the project. Common examples of WFH include a producer hiring a singer to cut a background vocal, or a songwriter being brought in to write a custom song for a company or brand campaign.

Work on Spec - Short for "Work on speculative basis". Meaning, work with no upfront fee or pay, with the intention that there will be monies that come from the work, and when/if the work makes money, one will make money.

Writer's Share - See "Songwriter Shares."